More Praise for *Irrigating India*

Sol Resnick's humanity and concern for others are reflected on every page of this insightful book. *Irrigating India* ranks with such works as V.S. Naipaul's *India: A Million Mutinies Now*, Alexander Frater's *Chasing the Monsoon: A Modern Pilgrimage Through India,* and Dominique Lapierre's *The City of Joy.*

—Norman N. Gill
Senior Research Scholar, Marquette University

India often elicits extreme reactions from visitors to its shores. Fortunate are those who discover the true essence of this rich and ancient culture. Sol Resnick not only came to appreciate India but gave the Indian people more in five years than most have in a lifetime. His captivating story is one of extreme compassion, courage, and caring for his fellow mankind. Elaine Minow Resnick's vibrant writing makes her husband's experiences in India come alive!

—Dr. Prem Sharma
Author of *Mandalay's Child*

I was fascinated by *Irrigating India*, especially because Sol Resnick wrote about a part of India that I know well. His descriptions of people and places made me feel I was right there with him. The example he set was a refreshing contrast to the image of the English "sahib"—and thus a surprise to many of his Indian counterparts.

—Bill Whitcomb
Agricultural Missionary in Central India, 1950-1973

A tremendous story told with such warmth and humor that I could not put it down! It conveys the struggle to stay healthy, the process of adapting to local cultures, and the overwhelming sense of joy in receiving gratitude from people you help. Sol Resnick is able to find elements of humor and a poetic irony in the daily activities and chance occurrences that shaped his life. *Irrigating India* also provides an absorbing historical perspective on India. Having recently served in the Peace Corps for three years, this book brought back memories of my own experiences.

—Terry Sprouse
Water Resources Research Center, University of Arizona
Former Peace Corps Volunteer

Irrigating India

My Five Years as a USAID Advisor

To Sally —
A bit of history.
Elin + Sol

by Sol Resnick
as told to
Elaine Minow Resnick

Published by PB Publishing, a division of Printstar Books

PRINTSTAR
BOOKS

Affiliated Publishers in
Milwaukee • Denver • Vancouver, B.C.

Cover and text design by Deb Lessila
Edited by Maris Bootzin

05 04 03 02 01   5 4 3 2 1

ISBN: 0-9706531-3-1
Library of Congress Control Number: 2001089103

First Printing 2001
Printed in the United States of America

Published by PB Publishing, a division of Printstar Books
Milwaukee, WI

PRINTSTAR
BOOKS

5630 N. Lake Drive, Milwaukee, Wisconsin 53217
414-906-0600 • e-mail: pbpub@execpc.com

Affiliated Publishers in
Milwaukee • Denver • Vancouver, B.C.

To all of our family and friends
who have heard Sol's stories
and wanted more
and, of course,
To Sol

E.M.R.

Acknowledgments

Without the prodding of Sol's nieces, Phyllis Bartlett and Annette Bode, I never would have begun this project. Without the support of my SAGE writing group at the University of Arizona, who suffered through the first drafts of each chapter, I may never have continued. Without the enthusiastic comments of those few people I allowed to read it, Cheryl Pickrell, an English teacher at St. Gregory High School, my friend Ethel Gill, and my niece Mary Minow, I would not have had the courage to move forward to publication. Without Susan Pittelman, my publisher, and Deb Lessila, my designer, this book would never have become a reality. I thank my editor, Maris Bootzin, not only for her help, but also for her optimism. And, of course, my thanks to Sol for his wonderful stories and his lessons about hydrology, without which this book would not have been possible.

—E.M.R.

Irrigating India
My Five Years as a USAID Advisor

Contents

Preface

I probably heard my first "Sol Story" about India around 1960, when my first husband and I brought our children to visit their grandmother in Tucson. Sol dropped in to visit us at her home and entertained our five- and six-year-olds with tales of the tigers and snakes he had encountered during his five years working in India as a technical advisor. But I'd met Sol much earlier, in 1935, when I was two-and-a-half years old and flower girl at the wedding where his brother Vic married my first cousin Sarah. Sol, then sixteen, says he remembers that I didn't shyly walk down the aisle, sprinkling my flowers, but skipped down, tossing flowers high in the air. He says that that's when he fell in love with me, and that if he had been four years old, he would have dated me.

I think I fell in love with Sol the summer I was thirteen, when he came back from serving in the American Army in Italy during World War II. But Sol didn't wait for me to grow up. He moved to Colorado and was off to work in India before I finished school. Our paths crossed over the years at family parties, and Vic always kept each of us informed about what the other was doing. Whenever I came to Tucson, Sol came to call. And if Sol came to visit my parents in Palm Springs, I'd see him there.

We finally did date in 1976, after the death of my first husband. But Sol lived in Tucson and I lived in Los Angeles, a place geographically unsuitable for easy commuting. Sol, by that time a professor of hydrology and director of the Water Resources Research Center at the University of Arizona, wasn't yet ready to settle down anyway. He was still traveling all over the world on irrigation projects for AID and the World Bank. Sol finally did marry for the first time in 1981, at the age of sixty-three, a marriage that ended in 1993. My second husband died in 1992, and when Sol's niece, who was also my cousin, told me in November 1993, "Uncle Sollie is getting divorced," I replied, "Oh, if he's ever in L.A., have him call." Later that month Vic came to L.A. and called to give me the same news. I gave him the same glib reply.

Sol did telephone soon after. He called, and called again. But he didn't come to Los Angeles until May 1994. We made many trips between Los Angeles and Tucson until I moved to Tucson in December 1994. We married in April 1997.

My own interest in India began when my brother was stationed there during World War II. It was through his letters and pictures that I first heard about drought and famine, Indian fakirs and snake charmers, and learned such words as leprosy and elephantiasis. When I had to do a school project, I always picked India. That's how I learned my Indian geography and history. I was lucky enough to tour India and Nepal for five weeks in 1984. There I experienced firsthand the complexities of India: its wealth, its poverty, its colors, its smells, its blendings of cultures and religions.

I've heard lots more "Sol Stories" in the past five years. Stories not only about India, but about his four years of military service in U.S. Army Intelligence in Italy, his three years in Brazil, his work in Thailand, the Philippines, Israel, Turkey, Tibet, and other places around the world. But it was the Indian years, 1952 to 1957, that Sol calls the happiest years of his life, years that gave him a tremendous feeling of accomplishment, of being able to do something that made a great difference in the lives of others.

Sol is a master storyteller. I'm sure it's not only because his stories are fascinating, but also because of his enthusiasm; his delight shines through his words. He tells his stories in a very matter-of-fact manner, as if anyone else would have done the same thing. I doubt that. There aren't many people who would spend almost five years living in often primitive and dangerous conditions in India teaching irrigation techniques to better the Indian villagers' way of life. When he describes his years in India as "the best five years of my life," I like to tease him and ask, "What about the five years with me?" He blushes a little, grins a bit, then laughs and tells me that the five years with me are better, but . . .

Taken individually, Sol's stories and anecdotes are sometimes fascinating, sometimes horrifying, always interesting. Taken collectively, they paint a picture of India in the years just after independence as the people struggled to raise their standard of living with better food, education, and health. They describe an American program that worked because of the vision of two wise and compassionate Indian and American government officials, Prime Minister Jawaharlal Nehru and United States Ambassador Chester Bowles. They describe a program that worked because America did not simply give aid to India, it provided training for Indian villagers by men and women who were not afraid to go out into the field and work side by side with them.

I've tried as best I can to capture Sol's stories as he tells them in his own words.

—Elaine Minow Resnick

Chapter 1

In the Beginning
The Road to India

Marble Rock Gorge of the Narbada River.

The years I worked in India, 1952 to 1957, were the best
five years of my life. I knew the Indian people were
dependent on rainfall, but I had no concept of the true effect
of drought. The consecutive droughts of 1951 and 1952 in
central India were disastrous. A two-year drought had
occurred only twelve times before in India during four hundred years of record keeping. Famine in the villages and
overcrowded cities weakened the people, who became easy
prey to disease. The U.S. State Department established

1

TCM, the Technology Cooperation Mission, as part of the Point Four Program of the Marshall Plan after World War II. Later known as AID, the Agency for International Development, TCM, with assistance from the Ford Foundation, was to provide technical and economic assistance to developing countries. The AID program helped the developing nations and benefited the United States. Once a country began to develop its own economy, it bought more and more goods from the U.S. The program in India was very successful.

AID sent me to India and gave me a free hand and unlimited money. I was to design and build village irrigation projects to demonstrate ways to protect against the disastrous aftermath of droughts. Most important, I was to train Indian engineers and teach Indian villagers new methods of irrigation. It was a tremendous experience. You forget the temperatures that could reach 115 or 116 degrees Fahrenheit, with no air conditioning. You forget the exotic food. You remember the looks on the faces of the people you helped. Those looks stay in your mind forever.

I didn't plan to go to India, much less to work there for almost five years. My childhood dream was to prevent floods in China. It all goes back to when I was about twelve years old, growing up in Milwaukee, Wisconsin. Browsing the shelves at the public library one day, I found a book about floods in China. The librarian told me I wouldn't like it, but I knew better and took it out anyway. That book set the direction for the rest of my life. I always knew I would do something to help people. I decided then and there that I would help the starving people in China. I would become an engineer and stop Chinese rivers from flooding.

When I enrolled at the University of Wisconsin in civil engineering in 1936, I was assigned to an advisor. I expected an older man and was surprised when I walked into a small office in a trailer on campus and found a young man sitting, feet propped up on his desk, drinking a cup of coffee. He asked if I wanted any coffee and I said sure. He put me at ease. Then he leaned back in his chair, laced his hands behind his head, and asked, "If you could do anything you wanted to with your life, what would you do?" I answered by telling him about the library book I read as a child.

He thought for a moment and said, "You don't want to just work with floods; there is something much more important than flooding. Food. If you really want to help starving people, you don't just give them food. You teach them to grow their own. You should do a dual major in civil engineering and agricultural engineering." He sent me off to the Agricultural Engineering Department.

No one in Ag Engineering knew what to do with me. I told my story again and again. Each professor shrugged his shoulders and passed me up the line until I found myself in the office of the dean of the Ag Engineering Department. I repeated my story. He thought for a moment and said, "Why not?" He devised a dual major with civil engineering, which would take me "only six years" if I carried twenty-one credits a semester. I did it. Then I signed up for job interviews.

In 1942 Dravco, a civil engineering firm, received a multimillion-dollar contract from the U.S. Navy to build a shipyard. The contract specified that they run model studies, but as they had no one who could do it, they tried to hire

Professor Lenz, who ran the model studies at the university. I was his student assistant. Professor Lenz refused the job and suggested I could do it. "Sol is graduating and has been working with me for years," Professor Lenz said. "He knows everything about models that I know. And, if he has any questions, he can always come to me." I was briefly interviewed and hired on the spot. Just before the interviewer left, he handed me an application to fill out, a routine matter. I filled it out, including the blank for religion. I wrote: Jewish.

A few days later, I was called in to the campus engineering office and told that the company telephoned and said they were very sorry, but they didn't need me. I put my name back on the interview list. When Professor Lenz noticed I was back on the list, he called Dravco and asked what happened. They told him that they were sorry, but they hadn't known I was Jewish. Company policy said no Jews. Lenz asked what they were going to do about their Navy contract. They told him that they would rather lose their multimillion-dollar contract than hire me, a Jew.

My first job upon graduation in 1942 was as an assistant hydraulic engineer with TVA, the Tennessee Valley Authority. That gave me the opportunity to work with two of the best hydrologists of the time, Bill Ackerman and Ray Linsley. They introduced me to the field of hydrology, the study of all aspects of water resources. I volunteered for the SEABEES, the Navy's Construction Battalion, but somehow was inducted into the U.S. Army and spent four years as an Army counterintelligence officer in Italy during and after World War II. When my enlistment was up, I returned to

Madison for graduate work.

Professor Lenz knew of my growing interest in water and irrigation and, even though I was earning my master's degree in civil engineering, the university allowed me to take most of my course work outside the Civil Engineering Department. I took classes in geology, atmospheric sciences, and soil physics. In 1949 I became an assistant professor at Colorado A & M, later renamed Colorado State University, to teach and work on my doctoral dissertation.

While I was at Colorado A & M in 1952, I heard about an opportunity to go to Israel as a U.S. technical advisor for AID. It sounded like a job made just for me. I quickly signed up, packed all my belongings, and traveled to Milwaukee to say goodbye to my family. I was ready to leave for Israel, when the AID office called me to say that AID couldn't send any Jews to work in Israel. They said I could go to India or Argentina instead. I thought about it. I decided on India. After all, India was close to China, and I knew how much they needed to learn modern irrigation techniques. Despite my mother's claim that she would disown me if I went anywhere but Israel, I stuck with my decision and signed on for two years. I stayed almost five as a member of the first group of AID advisors to go to India. There were ninety-six people in the field group, representing various disciplines such as public health, education, and agriculture. My mission was to train Indian engineers and develop small irrigation projects to help the Indian villagers grow more food of their own.

The success of an AID program in each country

depended chiefly on the interests and abilities of the U.S. ambassador to that country and the local government. Fortunately, the U.S. ambassador to India was Chester Bowles, and India's prime minister was Jawaharlal Nehru. These incredible human beings set up thirty-two demonstration project areas throughout India; each project area contained approximately five hundred villages. Because Bowles and Nehru knew that local involvement was key, they chose to pay India's required half-share of the cost with local labor. The U.S. provided materials as its share.

Four of the thirty-two project areas were in the State of Madhya Pradesh in the heart of India. Four of us were sent to Nagpur, then the capital of Madhya Pradesh. Frank Shepard and Paul Creech taught improved methods of farming. Frank Bell set up boys' clubs similar to our 4-H Clubs. I was there as an irrigation engineer to teach and set up small village projects.

Although there were supposed to be twelve irrigation engineers in the program, they couldn't lure anyone but me. For the next three years, I was the only one in India. Finally, a second arrived, an older man who had retired after many years of work for the U.S. Bureau of Reclamation. After barely surviving a week in the field with me, he said, "This fieldwork is only for young people," and served his two-year stint for AID at a desk in New Delhi designing large dams and irrigation projects.

Before traveling to India, our group studied for two months at a school in Washington, D.C. We learned not only the history and culture of the area to which we were posted, but the language as well. I learned to speak Hindi, only one of the sixteen or so major languages recognized by the Indian government. Actually, there are about four hundred different languages in India and even more subdialects. When I finally reached Madhya Pradesh, I learned that little Hindi was spoken there. I had to learn to speak Marathi.

I left for India a bachelor, carrying one suitcase and a couple of old footlockers filled with engineering handbooks and manuals. My plane landed in Bombay where I had a one-day layover before flying on to New Delhi, one day to see some of Bombay. A line of waiting rickshaws stretched outside my hotel, The Taj of India. I thought, "What a good chance to practice my Hindi," and waved to the first driver in line. Slowly speaking my newly acquired Hindi, I carefully explained that I wanted to take a ride around the city to see the sights. The driver didn't understand me. I tried to make myself understood again and again, not realizing that the people of Bombay don't speak Hindi, they speak Marathi. Finally, with a perfect British accent, the rickshaw driver asked, "Do you happen to speak English?"

He was delighted to take me on a tour of the city and asked why I was in India. When I told him I was with the U.S. government and going to Nagpur, he sadly shook his head. People in Bombay consider Nagpur to be the end of the world. We stopped twice for coffee on our tour and spent a few hours together. Back at the hotel, I asked how much I owed him. I figured that two hours at ten dollars an hour would be a reasonable amount and was ready to hand him one hundred rupees. A rupee was then worth about twenty-one cents. He said the price was four rupees an hour, and two hours were eight rupees. But, he said, we stopped for coffee twice and the fare should be less. When I gave him ten rupees, he was overwhelmed.

The next day I flew to New Delhi. I was first taken to the medical clinic where I got enough shots to, with luck, prevent any diseases I might encounter. The next stop was the embassy where I met many people, including the comptroller who was in charge of our funds. I met the people in charge of human relations who gave me information about the areas in which I would be working. The information was suspect since they had never been there themselves. Everyone I spoke to seemed to have the same opinion of Nagpur as my Bombay rickshaw driver. It was not like New Delhi, Bangalore, or Madras, all good places to live. It was the end of the world.

Nagpur became my base of operations for projects all over India. Maybe it was a good thing I didn't know what life would be like in Nagpur. Maybe it was a good thing I didn't know what it would be like living in a tent beside a small Indian village. Maybe it was a good thing I didn't know about the strange things I would eat in the tribal villages. Maybe it was a good thing I didn't know about the disease, the poverty, the tigers, snakes, and other wild animals that populated India. Maybe it was a good thing I didn't know what each day at the office might bring. Innocent of all that, I was on my way to Nagpur, my home for almost five years.

Chapter 2

Life in Nagpur
Not the End of the World

Getting a haircut in Nagpur.
Sol's barber is the first on the left.

Geographically, Nagpur, formerly the capital of the State of Madhya Pradesh, sits in the center of India. The main east-west highway and the railroad between Bombay and Calcutta run through it as well as the main north-south road from New Delhi to Madras. A Nagpur guide published twenty-five years later in 1977 describes the city:

> *Welcome, dear tourists, to the city of Nagpur —*
> *a city where you could lead a carefree life which*

> *enjoy all the advantages of the machine age yet,*
> *the machineness of life is absent here. You feel*
> *yourself when you notice that you are far away*
> *from the madding crowd, the monotony of life,*
> *the clog clog of machines, the whizzing trains,*
> *the blaring horns and sirens and the likes.*
> *Extremity in climate, living antiquity...*
> *is Nagpur.*
>
> *...(P)eople here are very urbane and hospitable.*
> *Yet on occasions they are as volatile and at times*
> *as nasty as anybody.*
>
> *...The climate of the region is characterized by*
> *hot burning summer, fairly distributed rainfall*
> *and a cold winter. The hot season is generally*
> *from April to mid-June and the average maxi-*
> *mum temperature is 37 C (98 F) [the maximum*
> *so far recorded is 47 C (116 F)].*

It was evening and, as the pilot began his descent into Nagpur, I couldn't see anything below but trees. I prayed the pilot knew where he was going. The old U.S. Army Dakota, now owned by Air India, skimmed low over the jungle to land on an invisible runway and deliver the mail and me to Nagpur.

Nagpur in 1952 was a city of about three-quarters of a million people. A representative of India's Community Development Program met me at the airport and checked me into Nagpur's finest hotel, the Hotel Mount. It was late, I was tired, and I went quickly to bed. I turned off the lights and settled in. It was not long before I heard the faint patter of little feet. When the little feet walked across my face, I jumped up and turned the lights back on. The room swarmed with cockroaches, scurrying as fast as they could back to their dark corners. I pulled on my pants and went down to the desk to ask for four big pans from the kitchen. Back upstairs, I put a pan under each leg of the bed and filled the pans with water. As roaches don't swim, I was safe for the rest of the night, but resolved that I wouldn't stay there for even one more night.

Because of its central location, Nagpur had been home to the main British Army camp, now abandoned. A major base, the camp had been staffed with high-ranking officers, many of whom had lived in the Central Province Club, the CP Club for short. The club was now half empty and going broke.

When I got to the office the next morning, I received a call from the secretary of the CP Club inviting me to visit and see if I would like to live there. He picked me up and we drove to the club. As we passed through the gates, I saw masses of exquisite flowers, manicured lawns, and an Olympic-size swimming pool. We passed twelve beautifully maintained clay tennis courts, and I loved to play tennis. The clubhouse was magnificent with a bar, dining room, and dance floor for use when the big bands came to play. Best of all, there were large, beautiful, teakwood homes on the grounds.

The home he showed me was outstanding, with ten rooms, many more than I could use, on a beautifully land-scaped acre of land. I knew I wasn't going back to the hotel.

I was sure the rent was very high, but was prepared to pay it. When I asked about the rent, he said $400. I asked, "Is that for one week or two?" He said, "No, that's for a year's lease." He drove me back to the hotel; I packed up all my things and moved in immediately. AID furnished the house with locally made rattan furniture and air-conditioned the living room and two of the bedrooms.

Word spread that there was a new American advisor in town. I wasn't in my new office long before a line formed of men looking to work as my cook and driver. I interviewed about ten before I found Sidasio. Sidasio had cooked for a British family for over thirty years and spoke Oxford English. I hired him immediately. Then I found Harilal, who spoke good English and had worked as a driver for a wealthy Nagpurian family. The government paid them each a salary of a rupee a day. I told Sidasio that I would give him an extra rupee a day as long as I didn't get sick on his cooking. If I ever got sick, he was fired. I told Harilal that he, too, would get an extra rupee a day, but if he ever had an accident, he was fired. It was cheap insurance.

American canned goods were available in the embassy commissary in New Delhi, but Delhi was a long way away. There were fresh vegetables and fruits in the local markets. Since Nagpur was primarily a Hindu area, there was only one meat market. Chickens were tiny, about the size of a squab. Even a tiger wouldn't take on one of those little chickens. Tough birds, they'd scratch his eyes out. They were just as tough to eat.

The center of Nagpur teemed with people, carts, horse-drawn tongas, bicycles, and roaming cows. There were few cars, but those that were there made their presence known with their blaring horns. At night the shopping area was dimly lit by tiny, flickering lights strung on bare wires. The first day I drove my Jeep there to shop, the local policeman stopped me to see who I was. When he learned I was an American advisor, he quickly moved bikes and carts out of the way so I could park. He did this every time I went shopping. He said it was the least he could do for me, a man who had come all the way from America to help the Indian people.

Not all local officials were as accommodating. Many needed a bit of *baksheesh,* a small bribe, before they would do their jobs. I learned this lesson early when I had to apply for an Indian driver's license. One of the men in our local office told me that if I would give him some rupees, he would go to the proper government office and get my license for me. But that's not the way I did things. Why should I pay someone money to do a job I should do myself? I went to the local office, filled out the necessary applications, and waited. And waited. And waited. Finally, I went back to the office and gave the man the rupees to expedite service. He came back quickly, my license in hand. India was made up of all kinds of people.

When in Nagpur, do as the Nagpurians do. When it was time to have my hair cut, I visited the local, open-air barber-shop. I went to a big one, one with three barbers. No chairs, just barbers. Customers sat on the ground while the local foot traffic detoured around them. First, the barber shaved me.

That cost one anna. With sixteen annas to one twenty-one-cent rupee, the shave cost less than a penny and a half. Then he told me to take off my shirt and lift my arms so he could shave my armpits. I did as I was told, thinking as he lathered me up that there was no way I was going to take off my pants. He didn't ask. He finally cut my hair. The entire cost was six annas, almost eight cents. When I gave him a rupee, he was beside himself with joy. I continued to give him my business, but asked for only haircuts for my rupee.

Almost anything was available on the streets of Nagpur. Men offered to clean out my ears with small, probing tools. I declined. Hawkers sold cures for whatever ailed you including rheumatism, falling hair, and sexual weakness. I never asked what else they had for sale.

While tennis courts, American movies, and dances were available in Nagpur, some of the more important things, things I took for granted at home, were missing.

Running water was one of those things. There was none in my beautiful teak bungalow. When I wanted to take a bath, Sidasio and Harilal heated water and poured it into the tub. Toilet facilities were even more primitive. There was a toilet in the bungalow. It even had a teakwood seat. But under the toilet seat there sat a bucket. When I finished, a hand reached in through an opening in the wall, removed the bucket, and returned it empty to its spot under the seat. The hand belonged to a bearer, an Untouchable in India's caste system. When I was at home in Nagpur, he hung around the opening all day ready to work.

Things were different out in the field. After Sidasio and

Harilal pitched my tent, they dug two slit trenches for latrines, one for me and one for them. They put a forked stick in the ground next to mine to hold a roll of toilet paper. I noticed that there was no stick next to their trench and asked why not. Sidasio and Harilal looked at each other and then back at me. They said they didn't have any toilet paper. They said they used water and their left hand just like most people in India. I thought to myself, this can't be. I live with these two men. Sidasio cooks all my food. I told them that in the future I would provide them with all the toilet paper they could use and bought it by the case.

Sometimes when traveling to a project, if I was lucky, I spent the night in one of the old circuit houses built all over the country by the British to house their traveling officers. Bearers there provided cooling on hot nights. Large pads four feet wide hung from the ceilings with ropes attached. The rope fed through a hole to the outside, and a bearer pulled the rope up and down, moving the pads like giant fans. The bearer tied the rope onto his foot, sat down on the ground or porch, and kept his foot moving through the night. Somehow, he kept it moving even in his sleep.

Naturally, there weren't any moving fans out in the field. On a really hot night, I couldn't stand it inside my tent. Harilal and Sidasio carried my cot and mosquito netting outside, and I devised my own cooling system using a bucket of water and two large towels. I soaked one towel in the bucket and, after I crawled into bed, laid it over my body. I would get so cold that I would shiver. It was wonderful. Cool and comfortable, I'd fall quickly to sleep. When I awoke hot and sweating again, I'd cover myself with the new wet towel, put the old one in the bucket, shiver, and go back to sleep.

In the villages, Indians didn't use toothbrushes. They brushed their teeth by chewing spearmint-flavored twigs from the local neem trees. Within six months, I was doing the same. Then there was the day I developed a terrible toothache and needed immediate care. There was no time to fly to Delhi. I went to the local dentist and sat in his chair. He operated his drill with a foot pump. It was a slow process. It was even slower than it should have been because the string running over the pulleys on the drill was full of knots. As he drilled away on my tooth, the string broke again and again. Wordlessly, he'd tie a new knot and drill on.

There was little else I could do for dental care over the next five years but return to him. When I moved to Tucson, I made an appointment with a dentist. I'll never forget the shocked look on his face when I opened my mouth. He straightened up and asked, "Where have you been?" I explained that I'd spent the last five years working in India. The Indian dentist hadn't left any room between my teeth when he filled a cavity. My teeth now formed one solid mass. The dentist sadly said he had to undo all the damage.

Itinerant tailors knocked on doors looking for customers. If you needed new shirts, pants, underwear, or pajamas, you invited them in. They took your measurements, went home to make the items, and delivered them the next day. Prices were incredibly low. I was at Frank Shepard's house one day when there was a knock at the door. Frankie, his four-year-old son who was quicker to learn Marathi than the adults, translated for his parents while they ordered new clothing for the family.

Sidasio cooked on a wood-burning cooking stove in the kitchen. AID bought me a refrigerator that I kept in the living room. My dirty clothes were picked up by the club laundry boy on his water buffalo and washed by machine at the club. When we were out in the field, Sidasio did my laundry by hand in the river or village pond.

I did go to New Delhi periodically for meetings. Whenever I went, I had a list of stops. Of course, I had to put in an appearance at AID headquarters. They always wanted a report on how our demonstration projects were going. I might need to visit the Indian government counterparts of the U.S. Bureau of Reclamation, the U.S. Geological Survey, or the U.S. Department of Agriculture to locate copies of old studies that might provide me with data on river catchment areas or local rainfall records.

Other stops were for me. I made a beeline for the embassy dispensary almost every time I came to Delhi. India harbored so many diseases, we were scheduled to get booster shots for typhus, cholera, and other known bugs about every six months. But if I happened to come to Delhi more often, even just two or three months after the last visit, I still showed up at the dispensary door. The nurses greeted me with, "Sol, you were just here a couple of months ago." I told them I knew that, but it was better to be safe than sorry. I rolled up both sleeves and they shot me full of serum for whatever could ail me. I would be sick as a dog for the next few days, with arms so heavy I could barely lift them. But to my mind, there was no need to catch typhus or cholera or any other bug I could possibly avoid.

My last stop was the commissary. I brought my two large, metal footlockers, relics from my army days, and each time I came into Delhi, loaded them up with whatever I could collect. The workers at the commissary knew what I liked and put certain delicacies aside for me. They knew I loved the little Danish canned hams, which would keep out in the field. And then there were the normal little necessities of life like toilet paper, shaving cream, razor blades, and soap. I carried a list with me and brought back things for others in Nagpur such as Cuban cigars or Scotch whiskey.

I thought I would be the only Jew in Nagpur, but was very surprised to get a phone call on my second day in the office from Dr. Abraham, an Indian and the Chief Medical Officer of Madhya Pradesh. I had arrived in Nagpur on a Wednesday night. A local reporter had interviewed me on Thursday, and the piece had been printed in Friday's paper. Dr. Abraham called that day, introduced himself, and told me he had read of the arrival of the American advisor, Sol Resnick, in the local paper. He wanted to welcome me to India and warn me about local medical care. He added that if I was ever sick, I was to call him immediately. He gave me his home and office numbers.

Then he asked if he could get personal. I said sure. He asked if I was Jewish. When I responded yes, he invited me to Sabbath services that night. He suggested that since the services were at his house, I come early for a kosher meal. Kosher food in Nagpur? I was astonished. Their food, packed in iced chests, was flown in daily from Bombay where there was a large Jewish community. I learned that there were ten Jewish families in Nagpur. One owned a large textile factory; most held high government positions. The textile manufacturer had a daughter, Ruby, with whom I spent a great deal of time during my stay in India.

I was surprised that Dr. Abraham was in Nagpur. His family had sent him to medical school in Germany and expected him to open a private practice in Bombay when he returned. They were shocked when he announced that he was going to Madhya Pradesh to work. He reasoned that India had been good to his family and it was time to repay the debt. It wasn't long before he became the state's chief medical officer. I was happy he had chosen Nagpur.

I made many friends in India, both Indian and non-Indian. There were the missionaries, the British who stayed on after India's independence, government officials, and, of course, there was Ruby.

I seemed to have everything I needed. A beautiful place to live, a cook, a driver, places to shop, good medical care, a girl to play tennis with and take dancing, and even a kosher meal. Nagpur was not the end of the world.

Chapter 3

Government Officials
The Good and the Bad

Prime Minister Nehru visits Nagpur.

The Point Four AID program in India succeeded primarily because of two men, Chester Bowles, the United States ambassador to India from 1951 to 1953, and Prime Minister Jawaharlal Nehru of India. Other government officials, both Indian and American, were very important to my work there. They included Ravi Shankar Shukla, the governor of Madhya Pradesh; H.M. Patil, his minister of development; and Frank Parker, head of AID in India. But I believe the program succeeded primarily because of Bowles and Nehru.

President Truman appointed Chester Bowles ambassador to India in 1951. Bowles was the perfect man for the job. He truly believed in the principle behind the AID program, providing not only money but training to locals so they could learn to help themselves. The early 1950s was the time of the "Red Scare" in Washington. Bowles believed that the best way to defeat communism was not to build bigger and better nuclear weapons or tighten our political strings on foreign aid, but to help the developing countries of the world evolve into communities dedicated to freedom. It worked in India, which didn't turn to communism.

It was probably because Bowles was the perfect man for the job that he had to face a fierce confirmation battle in the United States Senate before he was approved as ambassador. Senator Robert Taft vigorously opposed Bowles's appointment, saying, "I cannot think of anyone who is less qualified to be ambassador to India than Chester Bowles." Citing Bowles's preference for spending money, he continued that Bowles's assignment to India was particularly dangerous because the Indians' "whole view is that we should give them the world."

Bowles barely survived the confirmation battle and dove headfirst into his new post. His timing was perfect. He arrived in India knowing he would have U.S. financial backing, and the year 1951 was the first year of India's first Five-Year Plan designed to raise the country's low standard of living. The plan's major concentration was on agriculture. Bowles saw how the U.S. and Indian programs could support each other. He went to Nehru with his ideas, and together the two worked out a program focused on improving farming productivity, public health, and education.

Bowles was a hands-on administrator, not afraid to do as he asked others to do. He traveled all over India and often could be found helping build a road or pulling in a fishing net. Bowles totally supported the AID technical advisors. Even though he left the post of ambassador in 1953, he returned to India frequently to visit our projects.

I realized just how much Ambassador Bowles meant to the USAID program in India when I compared notes at regional meetings with my counterparts in other countries. Unlike us, they spent little time out in the field. They mostly sat in offices designing large projects which for the most part were never developed.

Bowles was replaced by George Allen in 1953. John Sherman Cooper followed Allen in 1955. Both men allowed our hands-on, small-village projects and teaching to continue just as Ambassador Bowles and Prime Minister Nehru had structured the program.

That all changed when Ellsworth Bunker became ambassador in 1957. When he arrived in New Delhi and saw our projects, he exclaimed, "Americans working out in the field! We can't allow this." He began pulling the advisors back to New Delhi. I was happy to be going home soon.

Ambassador Bowles brought his wife Dorothy and three children to India. They enrolled the children in Indian schools. Dorothy Stebbins Bowles, known as Steb, was an amazing woman, truly interested in and involved with the people of India. I remember seeing her on the day of a huge cricket match in Nagpur. All business and transportation stopped while thousands and thousands of Indians gathered around the cricket field. Mrs. Bowles, who refused to have her own car and driver in India, was passing through Nagpur on a local bus on her way to the Gandhi Center, located about twenty-five miles south of Nagpur at Wadha. The Gandhi Center was a very unusual place. People came from all over the world to stay for a day, a week, a month, a year, or even longer. They entered the gates of the center and exchanged their clothing for simple white cotton garments. The center provided them with beds and all their food free of charge. They could spend their time at the center any way they chose: in study, in meditation, practicing an art, learning a trade, teaching, or simply doing nothing at all.

I was at the cricket game with Governor Shukla's party. I looked out and was very surprised to see Mrs. Bowles sitting on the ground surrounded by Indians. When I went over to her and asked her why she was sitting there, she explained that she was on her way to the Gandhi Center and was waiting for the game to be over so the local buses would run again. I invited her to join us and told her that I would be very happy to drive her to the center after the match. She thanked me but said no, she'd rather experience what the Indian people did and ride the bus.

The local buses, which ran from village to village, were hot, dirty, and overloaded with passengers, both inside and out. Riders perched on their bouncing roofs and clung precariously from their sides. You never knew what you might find in your lap as you rode the bus, anything from a chicken to a bicycle. That is, if you were lucky enough to have a seat. I went back to Governor Shukla and told him about Mrs. Bowles. He respected her wishes to travel on the local bus, but sent one of his aides to help her find the right bus and make sure she had the seat behind the driver, the coolest and least crowded place.

Ambassador Bowles developed an excellent relationship with Prime Minister Jawaharlal Nehru. Nehru, who came from a wealthy, high-caste Brahman family in Kashmir, was devoted to his country. He was an incredibly thoughtful man and, as Bowles, always interested in what the AID advisors were doing. Nehru knew each of us by name. Whenever he visited his friend Governor Shukla in Nagpur, the governor would invite the four American advisors stationed in Nagpur and their wives to lunch or dinner to meet with him. Nehru would ask each of us how we were and how our projects were coming along.

Nehru stopped in Nagpur one night en route to Madras, and we were all invited to dinner at Governor Shukla's. When Nehru asked Floris Shepard, Frank's wife, how her children were, she told him that little Frankie was sick. She said she had taken Frankie to the local clinic, but they couldn't find out what was causing his vomiting and diarrhea. Nehru, quite concerned, told her that Indian clinics weren't very good and she should take him to New Delhi so an American doctor could examine him. She told him that she would if Frankie didn't get better soon.

The prime minister stopped off in Nagpur on his return to Delhi the next day and we all met him for lunch at the airport. Again he asked how Frankie was. Floris replied that he was no better. Nehru turned to Governor Shukla and asked for a car and driver to take Floris home to get Frankie so that he could fly them to Delhi for medical care.

This and many other little things Nehru did showed his character. Madhya Pradesh was famous for its oranges, and they were commonly on the table when we had lunch or dinner with the government officials. During the hot season, tables were often set up outside, and as the Indians peeled their oranges, they tossed the peels on the ground. Nehru was at the table one day when this happened, and he got up and began picking up the orange peels. The guilty officials quickly arose and picked up their own peels.

The governor of the State of Madhya Pradesh, Pandit Ravi Shankar Shukla, had shared a jail cell with Nehru during the 1942 Indian Freedom Movement. When you spend every hour of every day with a person, you either become bitter enemies or good friends. Fortunately, the two, both wonderful humanitarians, became and remained very good friends and worked closely together. Having Governor Shukla on my side made my job easier.

Governor Shukla, always interested in what his four American advisors were doing, tried to smooth each hurdle we met. He told us that he would support whatever we did to improve the life of the people of Madhya Pradesh, and he worked closely with us. His support came in handy when I had major disagreements with the state chief engineer, Dr. Seth.

Seth did everything according to the book, the British handbook. All of the Indian engineers were taught to do that.

They knew that if they followed the handbook down to the crossing of every *t* and dotting of every *i*, they couldn't be faulted for anything that went wrong and wouldn't lose their jobs. All engineering positions were based on seniority. The only thing that could prevent promotion was a mistake. The engineers logically reasoned that the less they did, the better off they were, because then there was less chance of making a mistake. If they lived long enough, they climbed up the promotion ladder and could, if they were as lucky as Seth, become chief engineer.

Seth knew nothing about agriculture. As far as he was concerned, farming was for poor people. You dug a hole in the ground, put a seed into it, covered it up, and watered it. When whatever you planted ripened, you harvested it. Seth was angry. He thought I was changing everything. He was right. I was. The British handbook was outdated.

Seth and I finally wound up head to head in Governor Shukla's office. Seth complained bitterly about my innovations out in the field. He told the governor his side. I told the governor mine. The governor listened carefully and then told the chief engineer, "You do what Resnick recommends. If something goes wrong, I will take the blame. I will not fire you."

Seth still wasn't happy. He dragged his feet over every innovation for a while. He finally asked why I knew so much about agriculture. I told him that one of my first degrees was in agricultural engineering. Eventually it became easier for us to work together.

H.M. Patil, Governor Shukla's state development minister, was born in one of the villages in Madhya Pradesh. He was a very bright man who loved his country and its people. A Brahman, he married an Argentinean woman when he was ambassador to Argentina. As a woman she was in close contact with the wives of the Indian officials, women who had little or no contact themselves with the world outside their homes. I often sat with Mrs. Patil at Governor Shukla's, and she told me story after story of women's lives in India and the poor way many Indian husbands treated their wives.

Patil asked us to do a demonstration irrigation project for his home village and planned a huge ceremony for its opening. He even succeeded in getting Prime Minister Nehru to speak. Not only the local villagers came, but about two thousand people from nearby villages dressed in their holiday finest sat on the ground eager to hear him. Nehru stood at the podium to speak. All the other dignitaries sat behind him, including the development minister, the chief engineer, other high state officials, and the American advisors.

Nehru spoke in Hindi and the people called out loudly that they couldn't understand him. Realizing they only spoke Marathi, he turned and looked at the men seated behind him and motioned to me. I asked, "Me?" He said, "Yes, you, Sol. Come up here." I stood beside him on the podium and as he spoke in English, I translated his speech into Marathi. I later asked him, "Why me?" There were many Indian engineers and government officials who could have translated his words into far better Marathi than I could. He said that was just the point. He said the officials spoke a high-class version of Marathi that the locals wouldn't understand. He had overheard me speaking the local Marathi dialect to the village people and knew that I, with my village Marathi, would be perfect for the job.

Sometimes Nehru's daughter, Indira Gandhi, accompanied him on his visits to Nagpur acting as his secretary. As warm and friendly as Prime Minister Nehru was, she seemed to be the opposite, as cold as ice. She never said a word. She never said hello. She never said goodbye. Even her eyes were cold. It was rumored that she was anti-American and didn't approve of what her father was doing. Maybe it was true.

I worked with other government officials. Dr. Banarjee was head of the Madhya Pradesh Department of Agriculture. Dr. Joshi, who worked under Banarjee, was in charge of agricultural training, a major part of our projects. Because irrigation and water systems were an important part of the agricultural training, Joshi invited me, along with Shepard and Creech, to teach the villagers. Joshi and I became close friends and maintained our friendship even after I returned to the United States.

Frank Parker, head of the USAID team in India, was a very likeable man, intelligent, and very supportive of his group of technical advisors. We sent him monthly reports on our progress. Being a typical engineer, my reports were very thorough. I wrote where I had been, what I had accomplished, and what I planned in the future. After my third or fourth detailed report, I received a copy of a memo he sent to all the AID advisors. It said, "Here is Sol Resnick's last report. I suggest you use it as a guide for your future reports." When Parker found out that I had signed on to AID with a government ranking and salary as a GS11, he boosted me immediately to a GS13. I was very grateful.

My original AID tour of duty in India was for two years, for which Colorado A & M granted me a two-year leave of absence. Early in my second year, I was called to a meeting in Governor Shukla's office and was surprised to find Frank Parker there as well as Cal Smith, head of personnel for AID in the Far East. They asked me to sign on for another two years. When I said I had to return to Colorado or I would lose my position there, Governor Shukla offered to call the university and ask them to hold my place for another two years because I was badly needed in India. I guess he liked the job I was doing. I agreed to stay on for two more years and never regretted it.

Chapter 4

The American Advisors
The Big Swede

Sol lecturing to Indian engineers.

India needed more to improve its standard of living than my irrigation systems. It needed better farming methods, better equipment, better seeds, better livestock. It needed better healthcare, better nutrition, loans for small business development, marketing expertise. It needed all kinds of training and education. Providing these things was the goal of the ninety-six American advisors who worked in many fields alongside the Indian Community Development Organization.

31

Ambassador Bowles knew the kind of people he wanted as advisors. When asked how he would select a Point Four specialist, he said, "First, carefully test the specialist's professional competence, then his patience and understanding of human beings, then his racial and religious attitudes. If these tests are passed successfully, I suggest that the tester take the specialist and his family on a two-week camping trip, preferably in the rain with a leaky tent. If they all come through with smiles on their faces, the State Department can send them to India with confidence." Almost all of the first group of Point Four advisors could have passed.

All of the advisors assigned to Madhya Pradesh—Frank Shepard, Paul Creech, Frank Bell, and I—were involved in agricultural development. Frank Shepard and Paul Creech, both from Texas A & M, had doctorates in agricultural education. Their job was to set up agricultural training programs for the villagers. Frank Bell, an agriculturist, worked to involve the young villagers in programs similar to our American 4-H organization. He wasn't too successful and went home after his two years of service. Shep and Creech organized educational programs that were successful and stayed on as I did.

The subcontinent of India is large, with diverse rainfall patterns. There is always rain and snow in the winter in the mountainous north. Bombay, on the Arabian Sea, and Calcutta, on the Bay of Bengal, both receive sufficient rainfall. Sometimes it was more than sufficient. I was in Bombay for a meeting on a day when twenty-four inches of rain fell in twenty hours. In the few minutes it took for me to run for a cab, I was soaked through to the skin. It was like taking a shower with my clothes on.

In Hyderabad and Madras, located in southern India, there were two monsoon seasons. In Madhya Pradesh, there was only one, and it was critical. The summer rains, when they came, lasted for about three months, from May through July.

When the rains failed to come, people in the villages died. Paddy fields, normally wet with growing rice, dried up. The rice crop was lost. Instead of rice, the villagers would turn to a legume crop called *til*, or lentils, which, being drought resistant, required less water. Droughts had far worse effects in the villages than in the cities because cities maintained controlled distribution centers for food that was trucked in from other parts of the country. It was our job as AID advisors to develop village agriculture techniques so the people could survive unforeseen weather.

The native seeds planted by the Indian farmers were very tough and drought resistant. Even insects and disease didn't bother them. But those seeds produced low crop yields. AID advisors, along with their Indian counterparts, experimented to find new and better varieties of seeds that were both drought and disease resistant and produced larger yields. Shep and Creech set up training classes introducing these seeds and new fertilizers to the villagers.

The villagers also needed better farming equipment. Farmers used their bullocks, castrated bulls, for threshing; the bullocks walked over and over the grain, loosening it from the shaft. The process, as you can imagine, was none too clean. With the help of a missionary named Brother Eaton, we provided the villagers with levelers, plows, threshers, and blowers. Brother Eaton invented a blower to separate the seeds from the chaff that was far more efficient than putting the seeds into a big basket and tossing them up into the wind.

When the farmers grew more than they could eat, they sold the surplus. In the past they had carried the surplus to the nearest small city to sell on market day. But advisors in New Delhi taught them how to pool their resources and form cooperatives to realize more profit from their products. New Delhi also provided low-interest loans if they wanted to build a school, fix up their houses, or start businesses. The advisors ran a full-scale operation.

Since I was the only irrigation engineer among the ninety-six Americans, I was often asked to develop projects in other parts of India. An advisor in Hyderabad asked me to visit a small village there to study a possible irrigation project. The advisor, who looked like a Norse god, called himself a "big Swede." Blond and at least six feet, three inches tall, he towered above the villagers.

It turned out that the well water in the village was polluted, a much more immediate problem than irrigation, but one that was easily fixed. Since there was no wall around the village well, polluted wastewater flowed directly into it. We helped the villages build a low brick wall around the well and that solved the problem.

When the new wall was done, the advisor, who had never been to this particular village before, sat down on the wall, making it easier for him to talk to the five hundred villagers who crowded around us. They were fascinated with this huge, blond man. I heard someone ask him where he came from. He explained, "I was born in Sweden, but I had to move to the United States." They asked him why. He answered, "I had five brothers, and they were all much bigger than I was. I was so small that they were ashamed of me and they made me move to the United States." They shook their heads knowingly. I think they may have believed him.

Another AID advisor was stationed in Uttar Pradesh, the province just north of Madhya Pradesh. If Madhya Pradesh was considered the end of the world, Uttar Pradesh was in the netherworld. The advisor there, one of two African-Americans in our group, had a Ph.D. in ag engineering and taught at the University of Rhode Island. His wife had a Ph.D. in education. They had six children ranging in age from about two to thirteen.

His specialty was farm machinery and he didn't know much about irrigation. So when villagers in his area had come to him requesting an irrigation project, he called me. I took the train, because driving north into Uttar Pradesh would have meant a long trip on bad roads. The advisor's whole family met me at the train station. The children lined up on the platform according to size and each formally said hello and reached up to give me a welcoming hug. That is, all but the oldest. When I reached the top of the line, she gave me her hand to shake.

I stayed with the family. After dinner the children were told to go and do their homework and ran off to their rooms. They came back for a cookie-and-milk break and said good night to each of us, again from the youngest to the oldest.

The next morning we all met for breakfast, the children

and their mother neatly dressed. When breakfast was over, their mother said, "Time for school." The children said good-bye to everyone at the table, including their mother, and left through the front door. Their mother followed shortly after. The next thing I heard was their voices raised in the Pledge of Allegiance. I went out to see what was happening. Each child sat at his or her own small desk on the front patio in their open-air schoolroom, an American flag and an Indian flag fluttering nearby. The mother taught six different classes. The last period of the day was their music lesson. Each child played a different instrument. Their dad made sure we came back in from the fields in time to hear their performance.

The project was an easy one. There was a flowing stream, good soil, and all I had to do was design a diversion system. I designed it and approved it for funding by AID.

Indian livestock offered different problems. I was in New Delhi one day talking to one of our advisors who was the head of the Department of Animal Husbandry at the University of Minnesota. Most of India's cattle were sick and of poor strain, and he was trying to upgrade their stock. Of course, he was having a lot of trouble with the Hindus. Their cows were sacred and they liked them the way they were. They treated their cows like members of the family.

The professor wanted the Indians to stake their old cattle out in enclosures in the jungle so that tigers and leopards would eat them. Then he would replace them with a healthy new strain. "Let tigers and leopards eat our sacred cows?" The Hindus were horrified. They wanted no part of this idea. He had little success and was very frustrated.

We talked about my work with the non-Hindu indigenous tribes in southern Madhya Pradesh and how the tribal villagers did all their planting by hand. He had a wonderful idea. He would bring a bullock to the tribe and teach them how to use it for plowing, proving his usefulness as an AID advisor.

The professor arranged to have a bullock shipped to Nagpur. When it arrived, we loaded it into a trailer and drove it down to the tribe. People walked in from thirty to forty miles around for the joyous occasion. I brought along some of the new equipment we had designed for plowing. We harnessed the bullock and demonstrated to the tribe how much easier it was to plow the land. The professor explained to the tribal villagers how the bullock could work for them. He emphasized that they could use him any way they chose. Everyone was excited. He left, secure in the knowledge that he had finally succeeded. He had brought progress to the tribe.

On my next trip to the village, I asked the chief how the bullock was. The chief broke into a wide grin and said, "Good. Very, very good." I asked where the bullock was and how the plowing was going. The chief looked puzzled. It took a while, but I finally realized that the bullock was not very, very good at plowing but had tasted very, very good.

Still proud of his contribution to the tribe, the professor asked me repeatedly if I knew how the bullock was working out. I avoided the question as long as I could but finally said yes, I had visited the tribe and the chief said, "They liked him. They think he was good. Very, very good."

Unfortunately, the professor wanted more details and I had to tell him that they ate the bullock. He left for home shortly thereafter, I'm sure to seek psychiatric care.

Chapter 5

New Friends

Missionaries, Brits, and Ruby

Ruby (right) with friend.

I made many friends during my five years in India: European and American missionaries, Brits, and Indians. Many of the men and women who came to help the Indian people were so devoted to their work that they ignored their own welfare. First among these was Brother Eaton, a Swiss friar who was a member of a Catholic order that operated St. Joseph's Church and its technical training school in Nagpur.

Indian boys arrived at St. Joseph's to train to be carpenters, electricians, plumbers, and artisans of all kinds. Not only did the school provide free food and dormitories for these boys during their training period, but it even paid them for the work they did there.

When a boy enrolled in the school, the missionaries asked him what he wanted to learn. If he wasn't sure, they gave him a chance to try his hand in many fields before he had to make a decision. The length of time a boy stayed at the school depended on his age and ability. After their training, the students usually returned to their own villages where the church helped them set up their own shops to practice their new trades.

Brother Eaton taught metalworking and ran the foundry. Tall, with a full beard, and thin as a scarecrow, there was nothing he couldn't design and make. He was totally devoted to his students and his work. He couldn't have cared less if the kids were Hindu or Catholic or Muslim. All he wanted to do was teach them new skills they could take back to their own villages.

There was no way I could have accomplished a fraction of what I did in India without Brother Eaton. Whenever I needed a piece of equipment, I stopped by the school and described it to him, and he produced it or something even better. I could have ordered equipment for my projects from England, Europe, or the United States, but I preferred to have it made in India for a number of reasons. First was the cost. Making the equipment in India cost a fraction of the price that it would have cost to import it. A good example were gates used to control water flow. Gates made in England for a village irrigation project cost about $15,000;

Brother Eaton and I designed a substitute system that cost only about $500.

Second, our system worked far better than the imported gates. Imported gates have rubber seals that disintegrate in the extreme heat of India and have to be replaced frequently. The English gates were too easy for farmers to open at night, allowing them to flood their fields and use up water intended for domestic use. Our cheaper system didn't need rubber seals and prevented lowering the water level below a predetermined depth. Finally, not only was money saved, but there was the added advantage of having the Indians learn to produce their own equipment.

When I first came to Nagpur, Brother Eaton was teaching sixty to sixty-five students. Within a few years, he was teaching close to four hundred. He designed and made metal flumes, plows, field-leveling equipment, and siphons. He made small wheelbarrows to use for moving earth on the projects.

Brother Eaton worked with all the American advisors in Nagpur. He even produced canning jars for Floris Shepard who taught the village women how to preserve their produce. Before she taught them to can their extra produce, they had vegetables only during the three-month monsoon season. Afterwards they had vegetables year-round.

Brother Eaton's only vice was smoking cigars. Indian cigars looked, smelled, and must have tasted like burning rope, a far cry from the Cuban cigars I brought him from the U.S. commissary in Delhi. He was always happy when he learned that I was off with my footlockers to New Delhi, knowing that he soon would have a fresh supply of cigars.

But Brother Eaton's work became his misfortune. He developed blisters on his legs that would not heal. The doctors told him he was allergic to the toxic black powder he used to line his casting forms and urged him to get out of the foundry or he would lose his leg. He wouldn't leave and did lose his leg. He hobbled around the foundry, on crutches he probably made himself, until the church finally sent him back to Switzerland against his will.

Another man who put the people's welfare above his own was Brother Thomas, a German friar who had been sent by his order to convert the Muria Gond tribes of the Bastar District to Catholicism. He wasn't too successful. Brother Thomas had no problem getting the tribal people to attend church services because the church rewarded all who came with food and clothing. He could even convince them to go through a conversion service. But they were converted in name only. The religion itself had no meaning for them.

It was interesting to watch the reaction of the tribal women who normally wore nothing above the waist. After their conversion, Brother Thomas taught them it was necessary to cover their breasts with a piece of fabric. They did, at least when they were in the neighborhood of the church. As soon as they were out of its sight, they took off the cloth and tied it around their hips. When they came within eyesight of the church, they'd stop and wrap the cloth back around their breasts.

Church officials decided Brother Thomas wasn't doing a good job and told him they were sending him back to

Germany. While he was convinced that the tribal villagers badly needed assistance, he wasn't convinced that religion was the answer. He decided not to return to Germany but to stay in Bastar and continue his work. For this, he was excommunicated.

Brother Thomas truly helped the tribes. He did a great job marketing their wild animal skins. Whenever a tiger or leopard attacked a village, the men banded together to track and kill it with their handmade spears or bows and arrows, often losing one or more of their hunting party. Dealers from Calcutta would come to Bastar and trade a few pounds of salt or some brightly colored fabric or beads for some leopard skins. Brother Thomas got a far better price by collecting the skins himself and taking them to Calcutta to sell. He used the money to buy food and clothing for the villagers.

In return, the grateful tribal villagers provided him with food and lodging. But he really appreciated it when I was in the area because I'd invite him to dinner. I'd pull some Danish ham and wine from my footlocker, and we'd have a feast, often topped off with a Cuban cigar. We'd sit and talk around the campfire, solving the problems of India and the world, until the sun came up the next morning.

It wasn't just men who were devoted to the Indian villagers. Women worked as nurses and teachers in church hospitals and schools. The World Health Organization (WHO) sent women to work in field clinics in the villages. It was a hard and lonely job.

The six WHO nurses stationed in Nagpur were my friends. They were Europeans, mostly from the Scandinavian countries. The nurses lived at the CP Club and on hot nights skinny-dipped out at the pool. They often knocked on my door and invited me to go along, teasing me when I said no thanks. When it was really hot outside and I was home, they camped on the floor of my air-conditioned living room.

Every Saturday night there was a dance at the club with an Indian band that played pretty good American music. Every Saturday night the Brits arrived with their wives and sat down at tables placed around the dance floor. The men sat with their eyes glued to the front door, waiting for the WHO nurses to make their entrance. The men in the band spotted them first and played a fanfare as the girls entered. And what an entrance it was. The nurses, who wore uniforms during the week, had their Saturday night dancing dresses made in Nagpur. They all had good figures and dressed to show those figures off to their best advantage, especially to taunt the British wives. Their dress tops were cut so low that the men made bets to see if they would stay up. Their skirts had slits higher than seemed possible.

These nurses affected one tradition in Nagpur. During the summer, when the temperature in Nagpur easily reached 115 degrees Fahrenheit, the state government moved to Pachmarhi, the Madhya Pradesh summer capital. At an elevation of close to thirty-five hundred feet, heavily forested and green almost year round, it was a little cooler up there than it was in Nagpur. It wasn't just the government that moved to the summer capital. The wives of many of the British businessmen stayed there with their children all week. Their husbands went up on weekends. When the wives found out what their husbands were doing down in Nagpur during the week with the WHO nurses, they moved back down to the city and refused to go back up as long as the nurses were around.

It wasn't just the WHO nurses who were seductive. One day I got a call from a Catholic mission church in the tribal area whose water supply had become polluted asking me to come and build them a new domestic water supply. I spent ten days there, sleeping in a poorly lit, tiny room. A priest and about twenty nuns lived at the mission. After dinner each night, we retired to a reading room, better lit with lanterns, where we could talk, read, and work.

After dinner one evening I talked to a nun who seemed quite taken with me. She left the reading room early that night. I didn't think too much about it. Sometime later I headed for my own room. I was shocked to find her there fixing my bed and straightening out my things. I thanked her and sent her away. She was so angry that she didn't talk to me for a few days. Then she apologized for her behavior and told me that she felt that I ought to be repaid in some way for all that I was doing for the mission. I didn't need her repayment. Just seeing the good that improved irrigation methods brought to India was more than enough repayment for me for the time I spent in India.

Most of the British stationed in India returned home in 1947 at the time of India's independence. A few remained on as managers or assistant managers of British companies. A very few were invited to stay on and help organize the government of the new Indian nation. One such British family was the Hemeons. Judge Hemeon had served as chief judge of the British High Court in the State of Madhya Pradesh. Since the Indians had little experience with the court system, Governor Shukla asked him to stay on as the chief judge of the new Madhya Pradesh State High Court.

I met the judge in an unfortunate way. I passed the clay tennis courts at the CP Club on the way to my office each day and longed to try them out. One afternoon, shortly after my arrival, I quit work early, raced home, and pulled on my tennis shirt and shorts. I walked over to the courts and sat at a table overlooking a singles game underway on court number one. I sat there twirling my racquet, hoping someone would come over and ask me to play. One of the players was an older man who looked like anything but a tennis player. His white shorts flapped down to his knees. Long white socks covered the rest of his skinny legs. But he got to every ball and hit it back. When they finished the set, the two players walked up to where I was sitting. The older man didn't take his glaring eyes off me as he came up the path. He said in his very British accent, "We haven't met. Are you new here?"

I said I was and introduced myself. He said, "Oh, yes. You're the new American advisor. I'm Judge Hemeon." He continued, "Do you intend to play tennis here looking like that?"

My big mistake was that I laughed. I looked at him and asked, "Do you think I would wear an outfit like yours? I'm going to be living here for two years and expect to play tennis dressed like this. My shorts don't have to come down to my knees."

The club assigned a member to make sure each sport facility was properly maintained. Judge Hemeon oversaw the tennis courts. That he was irate was putting it mildly. I heard later that he brought up the issue of my tennis attire before the board of the CP Club. But the board members ruled on my side. They reminded the judge that the club was going broke. They told him, "We have an American who will be living here for two years and you're angry because his tennis shorts aren't long enough? Forget it."

The judge and I became good friends. If you were a "dear friend" of one of the British, you could drop by to visit uninvited. Just "friends" had to have a formal invitation. I had an open invitation to stop by the Hemeons' home at any time. While I learned the unwritten rules, I never bought longer tennis shorts and still played many sets with the judge.

The British members of the club broke down into three social groups. There were about twenty people in Judge Hemeon's group, mainly high government officials and company managers. The people in the second group were assistant managers. Those in group three were the assistants to the assistants.

Almost every evening Judge Hemeon came straight from his office to the club where he sat and drank steadily for hours. Then his driver half-carried him to his car and took him home dead drunk. Most evenings the British gathered in a circle of chairs in a lounge in the clubhouse for drinks before dinner. They invited me to join them. The judge introduced me to the group and I thought I'd have one drink and leave. I had my drink and tried to find a waiter to get my check, but someone else signed it before I could. I called the waiter over, ordered a round for the group, then took the bill explaining that I was hungry and going to dinner. The judge said I couldn't leave because everyone owed me a drink. I told him I'd collect over the next two years.

I did stop by Judge Hemeon's drinking group occasionally. One evening they were discussing what they would like to be in their next life. I was somewhat shocked when Mrs. Hemeon replied that she wanted to come back in her next life as a bull on the pampas in Argentina, a bull with her own herd of cows.

Mrs. Hemeon was a charming woman, a photographer. She spent her time photographing early cave art, trying to capture it on film before "collectors" bought the art and removed it from the caves, walls and all. Mrs. Hemeon had had polio as a child and was limited in her ability to climb. After three years as the faculty advisor of the climbing club at Colorado A & M, I could scale almost anything. I offered to go with her and scout out those caves worth photographing.

She'd wake me up at four o'clock in the morning when it was still cool outside, and we'd drive into the Mahadeo Hills near Pachmarhi. Caves in the hills contained rock paintings, some of which were ten thousand years old. Since we could cover only a small part of the area at a time, she divided the area into grids so we wouldn't miss a thing. I'd sling a rope over my shoulder and scale a cliff to reach a cave above. If I found any rock paintings, I'd drop the rope down to her driver. He'd tie on a rope ladder, and I'd pull it up and secure it so she could climb up. If the art was worth photographing, she would set up her camera and lights and stay a few hours. I'd go back to Nagpur to work. When she published her book in England of her photographs of the early rock paintings, she thanked me in her dedication.

I became friendly with another of the British, the manager of the Brooke Bond tea-processing plant in Nagpur, which purchased different grades of tea from all over India. One day he invited me to visit the plant and proudly showed me the processing operation. The last room he took me to was the tea-tasting room. Sixteen small glasses were set up on a table so I could taste all of their products. He said, "Come on, Sol, tell me which tea you like best." He gave me a pencil and pad of paper to keep score. I went down the line, jotting down my comments: too sharp, too bland, too sour, too sweet, too tart, very good, not so good. At the end he asked which one I liked the best. I indicated the very last one.

He thought I was kidding. He told me that at one end was their premier tea, considered to be the best on the world market. The tea on the other end was their worst grade, made out of the bits and pieces of leaves and cuttings swept up with the dust from the tables after the best was picked out. I picked the worst. So much for my palate. We decided that I should stick to coffee.

A most important friend was Ruby, the daughter of the Jewish Indian textile manufacturer in Nagpur. I first saw Ruby playing tennis at the club. Then a few nights later I saw her there again, playing bridge. She asked me if I'd seen the movie at the local theater. When I said no, she advised me not to buy a ticket for main-floor seating but to spend a little more and get a ticket for the balcony, which had dividers like an opera house and was exclusively for the upper class. I went to see the movie she recommended, noted the coming attraction, and asked if she would like to see the new film with me. I was delighted when she said yes. She was very nice, beautiful, played tennis and bridge, and was even Jewish.

Ruby lived with her family in a home that covered an entire square block in the center of Nagpur. Walls ten feet high surrounded the home, and I had to pass through a security gate to get in. I passed her home each day on my way to work and had thought it was a military installation. I was amazed to learn that it belonged to only one family.

When I brought her home from the movie, she invited me in. As soon as Ruby sat down, a servant came into the room to take off her stockings and massage her legs. This was definitely a degree of wealth I was not used to. Ruby and I went to the movies, played tennis and bridge, and went out together for the entire time I was stationed in Nagpur.

Ruby had married the son of an extremely wealthy Bombay family that owned about twenty-five percent of Malabar Hill, the wealthiest area in Bombay. Her husband, a pilot for Air India, flew the Bombay-to-London run each week. The flight attendants on the run were Eurasians, beautiful women with dark skin, green eyes, and long, dark hair. When Ruby found out he was having an affair on his nights in London, she took her two sons, moved back to her family home in Nagpur, and divorced him.

Ruby's father's family owned big textile factories in Bombay and Calcutta. As a young man, her father didn't want to stay in Bombay and started his own factory in Nagpur, close to where the cotton is grown. This gave him easy access to the best and cheapest cotton, and eventually he had a payroll of over twenty thousand employees. His factory covered four to five acres. It was a beautiful building, two stories tall with a parabolic roof. The offices on the second floor were enclosed and very nice and modern. The factory proper on the ground floor was open, with the weaving looms set far enough apart so he could drive his Jeep through and oversee the operation. He not only produced bolts of the finest cotton fabric, but garments as well, madras shirts that he sold to places such as Neiman Marcus. He paid his workers a rupee a day. He became an extremely wealthy man.

Ruby's two boys went to school with servants walking behind them to carry their books. She flew to Paris with her sister to shop. Her father tried to get her to remarry someone from a wealthy Jewish family in Bombay. But she wouldn't do it. She was happy going out with me.

When I realized she was talking marriage, I tried to tell her that I was poor. I told her that in America, I cooked my own meals and washed my own socks. I told her that I had a good job and lived well in India, but nothing like what she was accustomed to. But Ruby was positive that I would marry her. And why not? She was a beautiful Indian, she was wealthy, we had been going out together for almost five years, and she loved me. She argued with her parents who finally decided that if it would make Ruby happy, they would have me for a son-in-law. No one asked me.

Late one afternoon, a few months before I was scheduled

to leave India, Ruby's father invited me to tour his factory. He was extremely proud of it. As we drove through in his Jeep, the first thing I noticed was that there were no toilet facilities. Men went off to one side of the building and women to the other. The whole place smelled like a toilet. Maybe that's why I noticed it. I also noticed that even though injuries were common in textile plants, there were no first-aid stations. There were no eating areas. The workers brought along their rice and rice water, and ate it squatting on the ground. After the tour, we went back to the house for dinner.

No one said a word about the factory tour during dinner. Ruby, wanting to prove to me that she could cook, had asked the wife of one of the American advisors for a recipe for brownies. She baked and served them for dessert. I think that brownie is still weighing me down.

After dinner her father took me to his library for coffee. We settled in and he asked me what I thought of the plant. I thought to myself, here it comes. If I marry Ruby and stay in India, I can eventually be head of this huge textile mill and wealthy beyond my wildest dreams. But that wasn't what I wanted. I had no intention of staying in India and running a textile factory for the rest of my life. I loved my profession. I loved what I was doing.

What I said was, "I think it stinks." I meant the actual smell. He thought I meant the whole plant. His face flushed and he asked me to explain what I meant by that. I told him the factory was beautiful, and he was doing a great job, but there were no toilets, no first-aid facilities, no commissary to buy food, no places for the workers to eat.

He protested that his factory was the most modern and best in India. He said the workers wouldn't buy food in a commissary because it was too expensive. They brought their own food. He said some of the people in the office were trained to treat minor injuries, and if someone was badly hurt, he was transported to the hospital by Jeep. But, he continued, as for toilets, no textile plant had any. He suggested that I go anywhere in the country and visit any plant, and if I found one that had toilets, he would have them installed. He went even further. He said that if I could find a factory that took better care of its workers, he would make any changes needed to raise the level of his factory. We never talked about the plant again.

I don't think Ruby really believed I was going to leave India without her until I was packed and ready to go. She did visit me later in Tucson. Before she came, I rinsed out some socks and hung them in the bathroom to dry. She finally believed that I really did do my own cooking and washed my own socks. She never did remarry.

Chapter 6

Indian Village Life
How Do You Explain a Dishwasher?

Village women planting rice.

India is not a poor country, but it is filled with poor people. Indian villages were unlike anything I had ever seen before. Almost everyone was poor, but no one was much poorer than anyone else. The people in the villages of Madhya Pradesh were gentle people, intelligent people, fun-loving people who seemed to accept their lot in life with equanimity. Although their life often wasn't very long—the average life expectancy in India was thirty-two years—the villagers were happy if they had enough to eat and their kids could go to school.

Life in the villages was tied to the rhythm of the rivers and the seasons. You could drive for a hundred miles and not see one person. But when you reached a river, village after village lined its banks. Along the Ganges you couldn't tell where one village stopped and another began. If the river flooded, the villages were washed out. If there was a drought, there was no food.

There were three seasons in Madhya Pradesh, the cold season, the hot season, and the wet season. The cold season began in November and ended in March, when the temperatures began to build. While there might be snow in the hills during the cold season, the temperature didn't drop very much in the villages. There it might get cold enough to sleep under a sheet. The hot season ran from March through June, and the heat could exceed 115 degrees Fahrenheit. That is, 115 degrees in the shade. People prayed for the torrential monsoon rains that cooled things off from July through October.

If a farmer owned an acre of land, he was lucky. If he owned two acres, he was rich. The village farmers planted their crops in June just before the expected monsoon rains for which they prayed. Day after day the villagers watched gathering clouds build into great, towering shapes as the heat rose from the ground to suck in cool, moist air from the sea. If and when the rains began, there was jubilation in the village. Everyone ran outside to soak up the drops, dance, and give thanks to the gods.

During the rainy season, the farmers tended their crops,

carrying human fertilizer out into the fields and spreading it. They pulled weeds by hand. They were out in the field from morning until dusk when they went home to eat. As their crops ripened, they even spent their nights in the fields to protect the crops from hungry animals. As Hindus they wouldn't kill animals and had to scare them off. The villagers built bamboo platforms and spent many nights up on the platforms above their crops, clanging noisemakers to chase the hungry animals away.

When the rains stopped, the busy season began. I knew the monsoon rains were over when the fungus stopped growing on my radio. After the monsoons, it was time to harvest, thresh, take yields to market, and prepare the fields for the next year. The winter was a quieter time. During the winter, the villagers tried to cultivate a pulse crop such as lentils or peas. They grew vegetable crops around their houses and irrigated them by hand.

The villagers needed a water supply, usually a well or a tank. When they needed to dig a new well, they sought help from a famous local water diviner. The diviner was a rather clever but lazy man who figured out a way to do his divining from home. The villagers walked twenty or thirty miles to his village bringing with them carefully drawn maps of their own village. The diviner spread the maps on the ground. He made sure they included the location of every banyan tree in the village. Then he took out his old pocket watch. The watch no longer told time, but did tell where the water was located. He'd hold the watch by its chain and dangle it over the map, slowly moving it in circles until the watch began to shimmy.

"There," he'd say. "Dig there and you will find water." And he was right. He knew that wherever the big banyan trees grew, there had to be a good water supply. He'd make sure the watch shimmied over the biggest tree and sent the villagers home to dig.

Other water diviners went from village to village. They, too, knew the trick was to find a big tree. They would invariably tell the villagers to dig on the west side of the tree so that the women would have shade as they did their laundry at the well in the morning.

Different crops grew well in different regions of Madhya Pradesh. Villages in the north grew wheat and barley. In the east, they grew rice, both wet paddy and dry. In the south, they grew a mixture of grains. Farmers in the west grew cotton. Without irrigation, cotton farmers harvested one bale for each acre. With irrigation, they harvested about three bales.

The women of the village were busy with household chores. They cooked, washed clothes, took care of the children. They spun cotton, wove *saris,* and made clothing for the family. The women wore their *saris,* yards and yards of lightweight cloth wrapped gracefully around their bodies to form a long skirt, top, and even head covering. Their husbands wore *dhotis,* loin cloths loosely wrapped around them in a shape that looked like a baggy diaper. These had the advantage of being cool. The women usually gave birth to one child a year, but only about five or six survived in each family. Children were very important. As in most Asian countries, people need their children to take care of them when they grow old. It was wonderful to watch family life. If a father squatted down, before you knew it his youngest daughter crawled up onto one of his knees, his youngest son onto the other.

The children, who didn't have television, bikes, or store-bought toys, improvised their own toys. They'd build a low wooden wall around an area, fill it with sand, and try to throw each other out. Sometimes I crawled into their sand pit with them and they tried to throw me out. There would be six or eight little ones tugging on me, two pulling on a leg, several on an arm. Their parents watched with amazement and glee and, I'm sure, thought, "The British were never like this." If the children were lucky, they went to school. If not, there was always work to be done.

And there was *puja,* prayers. Prayers for rain, prayers for good crops, prayers to ask the gods to be good to the family. There were prayers for planting, prayers for harvesting, prayers for living, prayers for dying. Stone images and idols are considered to be living gods, and the people not only prayed to them, but washed them and fed them. Just in case the gods didn't answer their many prayers, or if people were desperate, they paid the local ash-covered holy man, or *fakir,* to use his mystical powers. The *fakir* shook his bag of magic bones and stones and chanted the proper incantations to bring the supplicant whatever he asked for, be it good fortune, good crops, or good health.

Hindus believe that if they live a good life, they will come back in a higher form in their next lives. Many villagers believed that life was better in the United States and prayed to come back as Americans. It was surprising to enter a village hut and see a treasured, yellowing picture of Abraham Lincoln or George Washington hanging on the mud wall.

The villagers had no storage facilities. When they harvested big yields, they dug holes and buried their grain in covered clay jugs to protect it from bugs and rats. Because they were Hindus, they wouldn't kill rats no matter how much of their food the rats devoured.

The Hindu villagers ate no meat. Their main diet consisted of rice, millet, and wheat that they ground and made into *chapatis,* small round flats of unleavened bread similar to a tortilla. They grew pulses such as lentils, peas, and legumes, which had a high protein content. They grew some fresh vegetables and fruit, including oranges and wonderful mangoes. They drank milk and buttermilk and made yogurt. The village women cooked everything on fires of dried cow

Village school.
(Note the cow dung drying in the foreground.)

dung. Not surprisingly, everything tasted like dried cow dung, but after a while I got used to it and began to like the flavor. It was the children's job to collect cow dung on their way to school in the morning, and they set it out to dry while they had their lessons.

Village life was simple. Politics were managed by the *panchayat*, the council of five elders who acted as judge and jury. In small villages, the only medical care was primitive, provided by the local medicine man. Holidays were a time for celebrating with fasts or feasts, dancing and singing. The villagers arranged marriages for their children, some as young as five or six years of age. This was a carryover tradition from the times when marauders came to a village and would rape any young, unmarried woman. The young bride would come to her future husband's village for the marriage ceremony, then go back to her village until she was ten or twelve years old and ready to move into her mother-in-law's house and take on the responsibilities of marriage. If a woman's husband died, she had to marry one of his younger brothers so she could be kept as a servant in the family.

I provided the village women with some entertainment. The last things I stuffed into my footlockers in New Delhi were magazines. I didn't choose news magazines to bring me up to date on the state of the world, such as *Time* or *Newsweek* or *Life*. I collected magazines such as *Good Housekeeping*, *Better Homes and Gardens*, or *House Beautiful* to bring the outside world to the village women. Women who worked in the embassy saved these magazines for me. When they saw me coming down the hall, they would call out, "Sol, I have magazines for you." I carried my haul back to Nagpur and took them with me out to the projects.

The magazine pictures fascinated the Indian village women. I carried magazines to one project area that was crisscrossed by rivers. I could reach it only by riding for four days on the back of an elephant. Many of these villagers had never left their village, had never even crossed the nearby river. If they had no conception of the world just beyond their village, how could they conceive of life in the United States?

After dinner I brought my magazines out to the campfire and the village women gathered. They took a magazine and sat on the ground, paging through, looking at the pictures. I guess they could figure out what a chair or bed was, but if they came to a picture of a dishwasher, they would come to me and say, "*Sab, Sab,* what is this?"

How do you explain a dishwasher to a person who doesn't even know what a dish is? The women lived in one-room huts and cooked in a corner or outside on an open fire. They owned a few cooking pots and utensils and some small wooden bowls, but ate off leaves with their fingers. How do you explain an electric stove, a toaster, a Mixmaster? They carried their water from wells or the river. How do you explain faucets on a sink? They washed their clothes in the river or at the well and left them to dry on rocks. How do you explain a washing machine and dryer? I did my best and the women oohed and aahed.

Word spread that the American *sab* had magazines with wonderful pictures. Women from the neighboring villages walked in to see the now-famous magazines. They sat in small groups around the campfire with the local village women who, with their new knowledge about the outside world, explained the intricacies of the modern American kitchen to their friends who also oohed and aahed. But the new women couldn't believe what they were hearing. The local women would call out, "*Sab, Sab,* come here and tell about the dishwasher to my friend. She does not believe me." And I moved from group to group in response to "*Sab, Sab,*" and explained again and again how a dishwasher worked.

Chapter 7

Tribal Villages
Going Back in Time

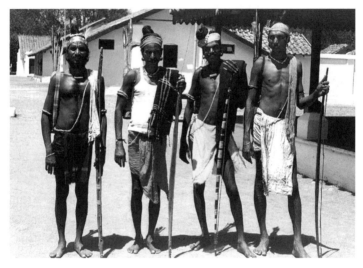

*Sol's protection squad armed with
spears, bows, and arrows.*

I never knew India had tribes whose history dated back
thousands of years. Ronald Noronha, an Indian civil service officer assigned to Madhya Pradesh, called one day and
told me of the Muria Gond tribes living in the teak forests of
northern Bastar District who still cultivated their land using
ancient slash-and-burn farming techniques known as *dahia*
or *bewar*. The tribe burned one to two acres of their teak
forest and tossed their rice seed into the ashes. The ash

provided excellent fertilization, and for two or three years they harvested a good crop. Then the yield dropped off, and the Murias moved on to burn down a few more acres. Noronha invited me down to see if I could find a water supply and teach them simple irrigation methods so they would settle down in one place and not burn the valuable teak forest.

The Bastar District where the tribes lived was not part of my assigned area. I thought about it for a minute, wondered if I should ask my boss in Delhi if I should go, decided not to ask, and said I'd be there. It was like going back in time to another world.

The Gonds were once a regal tribe that ruled Gondwana, the Land of the Gonds, which later became India's Central Provinces. The Gonds speak a Dravidian language similar to that of the Tamils of Sri Lanka, and may have originally come up from southern India as early as the sixth century. Their kings and queens peacefully ruled their large kingdom until the Maratha armies pushed them back into the hills and forests of Bastar in the eighteenth century.

The Gond culture is very different from the Hindu culture. The tribes have their own language, gods, and customs. Hindus are vegetarians; the Gonds eat anything that moves. When I worked in their area, they had little to offer me except food. Each family had its own thatched mud hut, usually surrounded by a bamboo fence to keep out wild animals. The women cooked on outside fires, tossing everything into the same pot, never cleaning it out. Each day a woman sampled her pot and flavored it with a collection of herbs, giving the pot her own distinct flavors. The tribal children collected whatever they could to add to the stew, catching and chopping up lizards, snakes, field mice, and rats, which they considered a delicacy, and other small animals. There was no set time for breakfast, lunch, or dinner. They ate whenever they were hungry, eating off broad-leaf plates and drinking from woven leaf cups. They had no forks or spoons. They ate with their fingers.

Houses in a Muria Gond village are set apart from each other, and if I was passing through the village, I tried to sneak through the gaps so I wouldn't have to accept any food. But frequently I was caught, and the woman of the house would hand me a leaf bowl. I'd stir and stir her concoction, trying to find something that looked like a leg. I wanted some idea of what I was eating. I knew I had been in India too long one evening when I was enjoying dinner in the magnificent, clean dining room of the Taj Mahal Hotel in Bombay. The carpets were two inches thick. The damask-covered table was set with bone china. When I took a sip of water, a servant immediately refilled my glass. Then, after I received a message asking me to return quickly to a Muria village to check on a project, I began to fantasize about which family pot would provide my next dinner. I knew it was time to return to the U.S.A.

Food was not all the tribe offered me. When I worked with the Gonds, I lived in a tent that Harilal and Sidasio erected. I returned to camp from the project one evening to find a beautiful, young tribal girl cooking at the fire. I looked at Sidasio and asked, "Who is she?" Sidasio explained that the chief had sent her to take care of me. He continued that it would be bad manners to say she wasn't needed.

She brought water for me to wash. I washed, ate dinner, and when it was time for bed and she still hadn't left, I went up to her, turned her toward her village, pointed, and loudly said, "Go!" She looked tearfully up at me and went.

The next morning another beautiful, young tribal girl cooked my breakfast and was still there when I came back in the evening. We went through the same routine. After dinner I turned her around, pointed her toward her village, and said, "Go!" I thought that would be the end of it.

The following day I was out with District Commissioner Noronha. Looking very embarrassed, he asked if he could ask me a personal question. He told me the chief was very sorry that I hadn't liked either girl. The chief wanted to know if he should send me a boy instead. I assured him that I didn't want any more girls or boys.

Sex before marriage was natural to the Muria Gonds. There were any number of little blue-eyed blond children running about the village, probably fathered by British anthropologists and sociologists studying the tribe. Unmarried Muria Gond boys and girls of the villages lived in a communal building called a *ghotul*, where they usually spent their evenings dancing and singing. They paired off early and, if they so chose, married. But if they decided not to marry, they paired off with someone else. If a girl became pregnant, they no longer had a choice but moved into a hut together and considered themselves married and part of the community.

The Muria Gonds were delightful people, cheerful and lighthearted, usually laughing and joking, usually truthful and honest. Often when I laid out a project for them, I found that a few of the men were missing. I asked around and learned that they were not "out" getting drunk, but "up" getting drunk. It seemed that the sap of one species of palm tree had a high alcohol content. When they had a longing for drink, which they frequently did, they climbed thirty or forty feet up into a nearby palm, tied themselves to the tree so they couldn't fall off, and drank the sap until they were too drunk to drink any more.

The Murias had a simple culture. They tended their own small gardens where they grew fresh vegetables, both to eat and to sell on market day. They picked fruits from the forest, set traps for wild animals, and collected berries, roots, and herbs. The men grew rice, millet, and lentils in their small, cultivated fields. Once they began to use simple irrigation methods, they harvested nine hundred pounds of rice to the acre rather than four hundred pounds. With their larger crops, they set up cooperatives to sell their excess yields to buyers in Raipur and had money left over to improve their schools and healthcare facilities.

The men hunted with homemade bows, arrows, and spears. They formed an armed guard to protect me from tigers and leopards when I went out to look at possible sites for irrigation projects in the surrounding forest. They also acted as my crew when I surveyed an area. I had to be careful to focus on the surveying rod they steadied with one hand and ignore the bow and arrow they held in the other.

A couple of photojournalists, Tony and Dickey Chapelle, came to photograph and write a story about India's Community Development Program for *National Geographic* magazine. They asked an official of the program in New Delhi where to start. He said, "Go visit our aborigines. They're an example to all of us. See what's happening among the Muria Gond tribe in Bastar District, for instance. It will be a hard trip to a place where visitors rarely go. But you will be welcome."

The Chapelles contacted Ronald Noronha and drove down into Bastar, a hard, eleven-day trip from New Delhi. Frank Bell and I joined them in Bhirlinga, a Muria Gond village that was one of my demonstration project areas. They questioned the villagers, who described the U.S. program of technical assistance to the Chapelles in their own words through an interpreter. We spent two weeks driving through the neighboring tribal villages. Tony and Dickey saw and photographed the changes our program had made to tribal village life. They listened as the people told them that their rice crop was the best they had ever grown. Before irrigation, they often went hungry, but now had enough rice for two or even three meals each day.

The Chapelles took a photo of a woman drawing water from a new village well. She told them they now had enough water to drink all year without getting sick from it. They visited new schools and the new medical clinic, and they shopped with the now-prosperous villagers on market day in Jagdalpur, a town of fifteen thousand people twelve miles away.

While we were driving between villages one day, I saw

two hardworking young tribal men dipping water from a stream with a bucket on a long stick and carrying it almost a half mile to water their garden crop. I stopped the Jeep and drew a plan for them with a stick in the dirt, showing them how they could build an earth dam to trap the water and divert it directly to the field. We passed the area again a few days later and watched them building the earth dam exactly where I said it should be.

The Chapelles asked if the villagers had resisted the new growing methods. The villagers were surprised by the question. They answered the question this way: "Nobody ordered us to do anything, so why should we resist? Some of our leader's friends said several seasons ago that we should try raising part of our crop by the new way. We did and it grew better. So, of course, we changed." The tribal villagers were a wise people, quick to learn. The article appeared in the April 1956 *National Geographic* magazine, a good report of a good project.

Chapter 8

My Work in India
Wheelbarrows and Shovels

Constructing a diversion project.

In the beginning, it was difficult to get demonstration irrigation projects going. After a while, I had more work than I could handle. At first the Indian villagers didn't trust the American advisors. They thought we were out to take advantage of them, just like the British. The villagers said they didn't need our help. But once we completed some projects, bringing water and increased crop yields to a few villages, the word spread and we were in demand. Soon I'd drive down a small road and five hundred villagers would block my way. They'd call out, "*Sab, Sab,* why do you build projects for everyone else but us?" They forgot they'd said no thanks.

My first step was to approve or disapprove a project. I looked at the possible water sources and the soil composition. If there was a good water supply and the soil and drainage were good, I'd check out the land ownership. I made it a practice only to approve irrigation projects for AID financing that benefited large groups of people. If the land to be improved belonged to only one or two wealthy families, I felt they could pay for the projects themselves, not have the American government do it for them. That meant I had to drive to Raipur, Akola, or one of the other regional district centers, the equivalent of a county seat, to check the records to see who really owned the land.

After recommending approval of a demonstration project, I moved out into the field, usually just outside the village closest to the project. Harilal and Sidasio pitched our tents, dug a couple of slit trenches, and moved us in. With nothing but lantern light at night, it was early to bed and early to rise the next morning.

Training Indian engineers in irrigation methods was the most important part of a demonstration project. Our job in India was not just to build systems for the Indians, but to teach them how to do it. I always had ten or twelve Indian engineers trailing after me. They weren't happy to be assigned to me because I mainly designed small irrigation projects. They preferred working on big projects that they considered important and prestigious, such as dams or bridges. While they were very bright, and very well trained, only a few of my student engineers were hard working and interested. They still believed that they would be promoted if they followed the British handbook and didn't make any mistakes.

The Indian engineers wouldn't live out in the field. They moved their families into the largest nearby town and commuted to work. They got to work late and left early. They also went home at noon for a long lunch. A few interested trainees went on to develop village irrigation projects outside the demonstration areas. The young man who was my best and hardest working trainee eventually went on to become chief engineer of Madhya Pradesh.

I got to know some of the engineering trainees, most of whom were young men just starting out on their careers. One of them, a Brahman, was older, quite a bit older than the rest, almost ready for retirement. He, unlike some of the younger trainees, rode a bike to work. One day I asked him why he was taking the training course when he was so close to retirement. He told me that he had to work. He couldn't afford to retire because he had six daughters. He had already married off five of them with large dowries, but still had one more at home with no dowry as yet. He was thankful that he could continue to work and provide her dowry so that she, too, could marry well. He obviously had no money saved toward his own retirement. But in India the children take care of the parents. If he married his daughters off to wealthy husbands, they would repay him by taking good care of him in his old age.

If a trainee invited me to dinner, his wife was nowhere to

be seen. Only men ate at the table. The children of the house ran in and out serving the food. I don't know if the women's absence was cultural or religious or both.

Beside the trainees, I also met some of the small town and city officials. I became quite friendly with Mr. Vaidya, head of the Raipur Demonstration Area, one of the four demonstration areas in the province of Madhya Pradesh. At his house, wives sat with the men at dinner. He wanted me to meet a young American woman who had married into one of the wealthy, high-caste families in the Raipur area. She came to dinner with her husband one night and told me her sad story.

She met her future husband, an Indian, when both were graduate students at the University of California at Berkeley. He wore western clothes, drove a good car, and had a nice apartment. The two fell in love and lived together, but he refused to marry her. He told her that when he finished school, he had to return to India and would have to marry whomever his family chose. But she was so in love she couldn't bear to be parted from him and wouldn't listen.

She told me he tried to dissuade her. He brought her books describing how hard life was in India. He warned her that she wouldn't be accepted as his wife. But she said that didn't matter and convinced him that all she wanted was to live in a small city in India with him. They married and had a child. When he earned his degree, they left Berkeley for Raipur.

He was right. His mother dominated the family and made life miserable for her. The family took away her clothing and books, gave her saris to wear, and treated her as a servant.

She had no freedom, no money, and no way to leave India. I asked her why she and her husband didn't return to the United States. She said her husband wouldn't consider it. He was under his mother's control and would be cut off financially by his family if he left. She was desperate. That night she sent a message to me at the guesthouse in Raipur, pleading for help to get back to the United States.

I went to New Delhi and asked Bowles's aide if anything could be done. He checked and told me that if I could manage to get her to New Delhi with the child, they could be hidden in the embassy, and he would make sure they got back to the United States.

I formed a plan. I usually didn't drive from Raipur to Nagpur at night. Even though there was less traffic at night, the road, though paved, was still dangerous because you could easily hit a wandering cow in the dark. In fact, I usually didn't drive it at all. Harilal did. But my counterintelligence training during World War II had taught me that the fewer people who knew of my plans, the more likely I was to succeed. I gave Harilal and Sidasio the night off.

Using a false name, I made a plane reservation for the woman from Nagpur to Delhi and returned to Raipur. The only time she was allowed out of the house was for a walk in the evening after dinner. That evening she and the child went for their walk. I picked them up at a prearranged spot and drove them directly to the airport at Nagpur, just in time to catch the midnight flight to New Delhi. I immediately turned the Jeep around and drove back to Raipur. No one even suspected I had been gone. Embassy personnel met them at the

New Delhi airport and flew them back to the United States. As far as the family was concerned, they just disappeared. No one knew where they went. No one had any idea that I had helped them escape. They probably assumed they had been eaten by a tiger.

Requests for projects flooded our office. Wealthy landowners who thought they understood the system went directly to the embassy in New Delhi, asking AID to build development irrigation projects on their land. The requests funneled down to me and I'd go out to look at the area. I'd recommend to the landowner what could or should be done and then, if the landowner could afford it himself, would advise the AID office not to fund it. If I said no, AID wouldn't fund a project. The landowners were obviously surprised. They learned that their money didn't buy me.

One wealthy family near Raipur asked New Delhi for help in developing an irrigation system. I stayed with the family and laid out a project for them. Every evening the man eagerly asked me how everything was going. He wanted to be sure that I was enthusiastic about his project. On the last day, he asked what more I had to do. I told him I had to go into Raipur to check out the ownership of the land, explaining that I only approved projects that benefited many people. He put his hand in front of my face and twirled his ruby ring under my nose. He probably thought that everyone has a price. When he saw that I was visibly angry, he threatened, "I can get you kicked out of India!"

I laughed and replied, "Why don't you do that. Back home I have an air-conditioned apartment, an air-conditioned car. Back home I don't have to drink boiled water from a pond.

Just go right ahead and get me kicked out."

I preferred working on small irrigation projects, working directly with the villagers where I could see the immediate effect that increased water supplies had on their lives. The villagers wanted to work on the projects. They were so eager to participate that I'd have to assign specific, small jobs to them. I'd assign one man to open a gate in the morning and another to be sure the gate was closed at night.

Ambassador Bowles and Prime Minister Nehru were at the opening of a demonstration project one day and heard two men loudly arguing over their assigned tasks for the day's celebration. I heard the argument, too, and went over to settle it. Ambassador Bowles and Prime Minister Nehru, curious, followed me. In Marathi I asked each man to tell me why he was angry. The first man said, "I do half of my job and then he says he will do the rest." The second man complained of the same thing. "After I begin, he says he will finish my job." It seemed I had made a mistake and allowed their assignments to overlap. I asked each man what he wanted. Each told me. Then, in my best Solomon-like fashion, I told them they would do the first part of the assignment alone and do the second part together. The men broke out in wide grins and thanked me over and over again. The ambassador didn't understand the language, but did understand the smiles on the men's faces. He told me I should have been a diplomat.

It was the villagers, not the government, who decided which projects they wanted the AID advisors to provide. Dr. Patil, the state development minister of Madhya Pradesh, would start the process. He'd send his assistants out to tell the villagers about the four American advisors who had come to help them. They'd tell the villagers to think about what kind of help they wanted: a new school, a well, an irrigation project, better farming equipment. They organized meetings among the villagers, Indian government officials, and the American advisors so the people themselves could ask for what they wanted. This was a democratic process that the villagers took very seriously. The villagers were represented by their *panchayat*, a group of five elders. The oldest man in the village was usually head chief.

Each village meeting was the same. Patil's aides would erect a huge canopy. Five hundred villagers would arrive dressed in their holiday best. Minister Patil would speak first, describing the AID program and explaining why we were there. He would tell them that the United States would pay one-half of the cost of each village irrigation project by providing the necessary raw materials; they, the villagers, would pay the other half with their labor. He would introduce the four advisors and emphasize that we were not like the British, who built for themselves, but were there to do what the people wanted.

Usually the first thing the villagers asked for was a steady water supply. When rainfall levels were low, many village wells went dry, sometimes for more than half of the year. I looked at their wells and had an idea.

You could tell from the exposed hillsides around the villages that most of Madhya Pradesh sat on the Deccan Plateau, a volcanic area where thousands and thousands of years before there were lava flows of basalt. After the flows, the hills above eroded, and the eroded material washed down into the valleys. This porous eroded material was covered with more lava flows, and the eroded material between was trapped in what are called intertrappean layers. The process occurred again and again and, when it rained in the mountains, the water seeped not into the nonporous basalt rock, but down into the intertrappean layers.

I was sure there was water in the intertrappean layers, but I had to be positive. I took some of the villagers down into one of their dry wells, and we started digging with picks and shovels through the basalt layer. I filled small bottles with dynamite, inserted very long fuses, and planted the bottles in holes at the bottom of the well. Bottles planted, we scrambled out of the well as fast as we could. After the blast, we shoveled out the debris and dug a little deeper. We hit an intertrappean layer about forty-five feet down, and the water that was under pressure shot straight up. I climbed out of the well to discover that I had been declared a god in the village. Once I proved there was water in the intertrappean layers, it was easy to send out a diesel engine and pneumatic drill to deepen other existing dry wells.

During the monsoon season, the *nallas,* small riverbeds or washes that were normally dry, ran with rainwater. If this water could be saved, it could provide enough water for the village for a year. One way to capture and save the water was to create a tank. A tank was not what we think of as a tank, a large metal or concrete container; it was a village pond. The tanks, created by building an earth dam across the wash, could be quite large. Indian farmers had built dams in these *nallas* before, but their dams, not well compacted, became homes to burrowing animals, and seldom survived the first good rain. I taught them how to build dams that would last.

Before building an earth dam or almost any other kind of water diversion project, I drove and walked the catchment area or watershed that would feed the project. I needed to estimate the runoff efficiency. This was determined not only by the size and shape of the catchment area, but by its topography, geology, and vegetation. I had to make sure there was enough water for irrigation.

Once when I was exploring a catchment area for a project, I found evidence of an irrigation project hundreds of years old. The irrigated area covered ten thousand acres, much, much larger than the one thousand acres I was planning to irrigate. But I knew the catchment area I was exploring wouldn't provide enough water to irrigate those ten thousand acres. I knew the irrigation water had to come from somewhere else.

When I asked the village elders where the old canal was, they didn't know. That canal, built before the days of concrete, had been constructed of bricks and mortar. The elders showed me where they had found the old bricks they used in their villages, and I found remnants of the old canal buried under the sediment. The canal led to a nearby river that had plenty of water, but no surrounding land suitable for crops. Since I was interested only in small projects, I told the state engineer about the old canal and it became a state project.

Besides the size, shape, and other characteristics of the catchment area, I needed to know the average rainfall in the area and the flow records of streams. About four hundred years of rainfall records accumulated by the British were readily available, but it wasn't that easy to get flow histories. There were some flow records available for India's big rivers, but none for the smaller streams I was using in the demonstration areas. I had to get my own flow records. The formula for flow is Q = AV, quantity of flow equals area times velocity. It was easy to get the area. Simply measure the width of the riverbed and multiply it times the average depth.

Getting the velocity of the water was a little trickier. There were small bridges over the rivers or washes, some big enough for cars, some big enough only for foot traffic. I had staff gauges erected at the bridges and put in steel markers exactly one hundred feet upstream. I instructed the engineers and ag people to measure the flow every time they passed a running stream. One person would go to the marker upstream and drop an orange into the water. Oranges not only floated nicely, but they were readily available in this orange-growing state. A second person stood on the bridge to measure the amount of time it took the orange to reach the bridge staff marker. Information would be written on a form I provided. The collected data was used for designing the dam or diversion system there and in comparable catchment areas. Within two to three years I had a good idea of the stream flows. I also collected water samples so we could check the water quality.

With all this information at hand, I would find the narrowest point on the wash near the village, design a small dam, and the villagers would build it. We didn't have big

Village workers show off their new wheelbarrows.

earth-moving equipment. I didn't want it. I sent a request to New Delhi for wheelbarrows and shovels. Parker, my AID boss, asked, "Wheelbarrows? Why do you want wheelbarrows?" I told him I wanted the villagers involved in the project so they would feel it was their own. Parker said okay and forwarded my request on to USAID in Washington. Washington fired back with, "Wheelbarrows? Is Resnick crazy? Why does he want wheelbarrows? We'll send you earthmovers. Just tell us what you want." Parker told them why I wanted small equipment and they sent me my wheelbarrows and shovels.

Everyone in the village worked. The men did the digging, the women carried rocks or baskets of earth balanced on their heads. Some of their loads weighed sixty to eighty pounds. It was amazing to watch a woman carefully pick her way down a slope, basket balanced on her head, never dropping a thing. The children worked, too. It took three to a wheelbarrow, one pulling and two pushing. Later, Brother Eaton built small wheelbarrows for me, and the youngsters battled over the right to use them.

If we built the dam during the dry season, the earth was very hard and dry. The men went into the fields with hoes and chopped and chopped and chopped until they cut out a clump of earth for the construction of the dam. But you can't build an earth dam with hard clumps of earth. That's why their dams failed. An earth dam must be built with soft, moist earth that can be tamped down firmly to make it as waterproof as possible. I had the villagers build a low earth berm around a field. Then they filled fifty-five-gallon drums with water from their well. Bullocks pulled the drums to the field, and the water was poured onto the dry earth. The field soaked overnight. The next morning the women dug out the damp earth, which was now at optimum moisture for tamping.

I taught the villagers to build sheep's-foot rollers to tamp the earth. I'd drill about 120 holes in the sides of a fifty-five-gallon drum and fit pipes into the holes. The pipes stuck about four inches out of the sides of the drum. I put caps on the ends of the pipes. I'd wire the pipes together inside the drum so that they would stay in place when I filled the drum with concrete. There had to be enough little "feet" sticking out to make sure the entire area was properly tamped. Bullocks pulled the sheep's-foot rollers over and over the surface of the dam under construction as more and more dirt was added until we reached the proper compaction.

One of my concerns was ensuring that the villagers had enough water for their daily needs to last the year. Only surplus water could be used to irrigate the fields. With Brother Eaton's help, I solved the problem of farmers taking too much water. Brother Eaton designed a concrete box that we would install in a tank near the front edge of the dam. An eighteen-inch pipe went from the concrete box through the dam to the other side. The only opening to the box was on top. A tapered metal plug fit into this opening, and a pulley was rigged to the top of the dam so the metal plug could be raised and lowered, allowing water from the tank to flow into the box and through the pipe to the other side of the dam. The only time water could go through the pipe was if the water level was higher than the concrete box, and then only if the plug was lifted. If the water level dropped below the top of the box, nothing would come through the pipe. I made sure the concrete box was set high enough in the tank to ensure enough water for the village until the next monsoon season.

The tanks played an important part in village life. The people used water from the tanks for drinking, cooking, bathing, washing their clothes, saying their prayers, and, if there was enough, for irrigation. I remember one day at one village tank quite clearly. The temperature must have been well over 110 degrees Fahrenheit. I had been leveling the ground for a diversion dam and was hot and dirty. Near suppertime I walked down to the tank, level over my shoulder, at the same time as a farmer who was leading his muddy bullocks. We began talking. I laid my level down on the bank, and we walked into the tank together, the farmer, the bullocks, and me. I watched as he washed off his bullocks. I watched as one of the bullocks, relaxing in the cool water, raised his tail. I watched as the dung plopped into the water. Then I watched Sidasio collecting water from the tank as he prepared to cook my dinner. The farmer, still in the tank, said his evening prayers, probably praying for his salvation. I said my evening prayers, too. I prayed Sidasio would remember to strain the water through several layers of cheesecloth to remove the bigger pieces before he boiled it for twenty minutes. The boiled water came out like thick soup. I thought about how many of my daily nutrients came from the water buffalo. I calculated that by the time I left India, I had probably become one-quarter bullock.

Besides digging wells and creating tanks, we taught the Indians to build masonry diversion systems. We diverted water from rivers and washes into lined canals, and from there to the fields. I started at the highest elevation possible and leveled the ground to get a uniform slope in the canal to provide for gravity flow. Sometimes gravity wasn't enough and we installed small pumps.

Brother Eaton and I designed wooden gates to control the water flow. Gates are an important feature of an irrigation system. They not only can be opened and closed to allow water to enter the fields, but their size controls the amount of water available at each level. If the monsoon rains were light, people at the top might take all the available water, leaving nothing for the poor farmer with fields downstream. I designed the diversion all the way down the wash so there

Brother Eaton and his students testing a flow-control valve.

was always a flow, even to the lowest fields.

While gravity flow was the cheapest way to go, siphons made the fixed irrigation systems more versatile. I designed siphons for the system with Brother Eaton's help. If there was a really good monsoon season and the tanks filled up, siphons allowed the villagers to use more overflow water and irrigate to the far edges of their fields.

Again, everyone worked. The men cut rocks from basalt hills. The women carried the huge rocks balanced on their heads, gracefully swaying as they moved their loads to the project. A pregnant woman worked up to the time of birth. Then she'd ask the woman working next to her for help, and they would move off to find some shade under a tree near the field, put down a bamboo mat, and deliver the baby. The new mother was given the rest of the day off. She'd be back at work the next morning, her baby swaddled in a bundle at the side of the project.

The workers earned a rupee a day. They earned a rupee a day, but that didn't mean they were paid a rupee a day. The money came from the U.S. government. Each rupee equaled sixteen annas. One of the Indian engineers was assigned to pay them each day. The workers held out their hand as he counted out the annas.

One day I talked to one of the village men who told me it was tough to live on fourteen annas a day. I asked what he meant. Didn't he earn a rupee a day? He said no, the Indian engineer didn't pay them the whole rupee, but only fourteen annas, and the man paying them took the rest for himself. He said no one complained because they needed the work. The next day, I stood behind the engineer and watched as he counted out fourteen annas to each worker. I took him aside and told him that I caught him shorting the workers. I reminded him that the United States gave him sixteen annas for each worker and that he would pay them sixteen annas each day or I'd go to the governor.

The villagers were very proud of their new diversion structures and built them to be not only efficient but beautiful as well. They created patterns using various colored rocks. Often it took hours for them to find the exact rock to fit the pattern. I tried not to get impatient. They were so proud of their projects when they were finished.

The villagers were very religious people. Before beginning a project, they did *puja*, their prayer ceremony. Minister Patil or the religious man in the village offered up prayers for its success. When a project was completed, there was another ceremony. Again, the villagers dressed in their best. They draped flowered wreaths around my neck. I'd march next to the chief at the head of the line, my hand resting on his shoulder. I'd stand beside him as he started the pump engine if we were pumping from a river or help him open up the gates if it were a diversion project. We'd watch the life-giving water begin to trickle into the fields. We'd walk along the canal as the water flowed into the fields, with all five hundred villagers following behind. The people cried and cheered. Tears ran down not only the chief's face but mine as well. It was the greatest feeling in the world.

Chapter 9

Other Projects
Rainmaking and Spillways

*Harilal, Sidasio, and friend holding
rainmaking equipment.*

In India, I did more than just the village demonstration
projects; I even became known as a rainmaker. My interest
in cloud seeding began during my first teaching position at
Colorado A & M. A long drought in the late forties in eastern
Colorado had caused the cattle ranchers serious problems.
The ranchers approached Dr. Krick, former head of the
Atmospheric Sciences Department at Cal Tech, who had
learned he could make more money cloud seeding than

teaching and opened a consulting office in Denver.

Krick offered to seed the clouds for a fee, a fee based on the results he produced. The farmers agreed, but insisted that someone from Colorado A & M evaluate the results rather than Dr. Krick himself. A wise decision on their part.

I was asked to evaluate Krick's work for the spring cloud seeding in 1952. Knowing nothing about cloud seeding, I went to Socorro, New Mexico, and worked with the best men in the field, Dr. Blackman, head of the New Mexico School of Technology, and Drs. Irving Langmuir and Vincent Schaeffer from General Electric. They were on the cutting edge of cloud seeding, studying the development of rain-drops and snow in cold rooms and applying what they found in the lab out in the field. I learned as much as I could from them.

Then I went to watch Dr. Krick do his cloud seeding. I set up control areas to check his results in the seeded areas. When the time came to evaluate his results, I found that while both areas had slightly decreased rainfall, the control areas actually had a little more rainfall than the target areas he had seeded. There was a lot of interest in cloud seeding, and we were both invited to speak at the annual meeting of the state engineering society in Denver that year. About three hundred engineers heard us.

Krick spoke first, giving a glowing report of his success. I followed and, to the delight of the audience, tore his results apart. He was understandably upset. I stopped in the men's room before the long drive back to Colorado A & M. Krick came in and stood next to me. He seemed quite angry and asked, "When are you going to get out of my hair?"

"Soon," I replied and explained that I signed up with AID and was leaving to work in Israel.

In India, I heard of Professor Banarjee who was doing some interesting work with cloud seeding at the University of Bengal in Calcutta. I called him and set up an appointment to visit him there. When we met, he asked why I was interested in cloud seeding. I told him about evaluating Dr. Krick's study. He knew of Dr. Krick and was amazed that I had evaluated the man's work. When I told him I had studied in Socorro with Blackman, Langmuir, and Schaeffer, he was flabbergasted and could not believe that I had worked with such great men. I told Professor Banarjee that the men in Socorro would be interested in his work in India and called Dr. Langmuir so the two could talk and compare procedures. Professor Banarjee invited me to visit his cloud-seeding projects to learn what he was doing.

India in 1953 was still suffering from the two prior years of drought. I don't know how Krick heard about it, but Governor Shukla received a proposal from him offering to seed the clouds and bring rain. The governor brought the proposal to the state Water Resources Committee, of which I was a member. Krick proposed that if the rains after his cloud seeding were normal or below, he would be paid only his expenses. If the rainfall exceeded normal, he would be paid proportionately. Governor Shukla thought this was a wonderful proposition.

Nagpur had records of the daily amounts of rain for the past four hundred years. Only twelve times in that four hundred years had the rains failed for two years in a row. They had never failed for three years in a row. After two years of drought, the third year was normally a banner year for rainfall. Even though this was in the days before big computers, I was sure that Krick had this data available and had based his proposal on it. I told the governor and he said, "But what if the rains fail again? I have to do this."

I suggested that rather than hire Dr. Krick, they hire Professor Banarjee. They contacted the professor and learned he had already made commitments and couldn't do it. Professor Banarjee told them that I had "worked with the gods" and would be the perfect man to do the cloud seeding. After protesting that it wasn't necessary because it was going to rain anyway, I agreed. Governor Shukla wrote to Dr. Krick that his water advisor, Sol Resnick, would be doing the cloud seeding. I would have given a month's pay to see Krick's face when he read that letter.

Professor Banarjee didn't use the conventional ground-and-airplane approach, where silver iodide crystals are lifted or fired into clouds. He sent up hydrogen-filled meteorologic balloons with bamboo cages attached. Each cage was fitted with six aluminum canisters filled with gunpowder and a paste of silver iodide crystals in acetone. He calculated the prevailing winds, lifting speed, angles, and distances, and set the charges so that the silver iodide crystals were fired directly into the clouds. He used different-length time fuses to cause multiple explosions to be sure the silver iodide reached the cold, turbulent interior of the clouds.

I collected all the necessary equipment to seed the

clouds, which wasn't easy. The University of Bengal meteorology department supplied the balloons. I found a source for hydrogen. I had Brother Eaton make the bamboo cages with fittings for the silver iodide canisters. A factory made the fuses. I went to the state chemical supply office to get my silver iodide. The normal procedure was to fill out a requisition slip and have the request approved by the clerk, then take the approved slip to the storeroom and pick up the chemicals. I filled out the requisition slip and handed it to the clerk for approval. He looked at me, waited, and finally said, "The director is busy. He must approve this. Sit down." I sat.

As I waited, I watched other people come in with requests. They handed over their requisitions, slipped the clerk some rupees, and left soon after, request approved, to pick up their chemicals. There was no way I was going to pay *baksheesh* for expedited service. After I sat there for about an hour, the head of the department came out of his office and saw me sitting there. "Sol," he greeted me. "What are you doing here?"

The director was a friend, a fellow member of the CP Club. We often played tennis together. I told him that I had handed my requisition slip for silver iodide to his clerk who told me his director had to approve it. The director gave his clerk a look that would kill and invited me into his own office for coffee. He then excused himself and went out to "talk" to his clerk. The clerk went off to get the silver iodide for me. I never had to wait again. I never had to get my own chemicals from the storeroom. All I had to do was walk into the office with my request, and the clerk would run to get whatever I wanted.

Before the big day, I experimented as much as I could. I simulated the seeding and made sure I could gauge the proper angles and lifts. I watched the skies closely to determine the optimum time to release my balloons. The day came. A large group of officials, including Governor Shukla, department heads, staff, reporters, and many curious people who had heard of the seeding, gathered about ten miles upwind of Nagpur to watch. I checked out the winds and sent up a few small trial balloons to make sure I had the right angle. Then I released the real balloons carrying the silver iodide canisters and they fired right on cue. We hurried back into town and, just as we entered Nagpur, the largest raindrops I've ever seen began to fall. I was the conquering hero who had brought the rain.

Now that I was a proven rainmaker, towns and villages throughout the state flooded me with cloud-seeding requests. They even called from places where it was already raining. The people said, "Why do you make it rain only in Nagpur?" No one wanted to be left out. But there was one thing I always did before I traveled around Madhya Pradesh setting off my balloons and doing my rain dance. I checked the local weather forecasts.

One project I didn't approve brought home to me the contrast between Indian poverty and Indian wealth. It started when the Maharajah of Gwalior requested a large project. Before India's independence, Gwalior was a state in the Indian Union. After independence, it became a district in northwest Madhya Pradesh. The maharajah was a phenomenally wealthy man. British rule had added to his wealth. The British knew how to take over a country. They wouldn't fight the maharajahs who ruled their separate states, they simply made sure that the maharajahs got richer. The British wanted two things in India: raw materials, such as cotton and iron ore, and a market in which to sell their finished products. Even though the people in India were poor, there were so many of them that India provided a good market for British goods.

When Gandhi and Nehru planned the new India, they were clever. They took a page from the British book. They integrated the independent states not by war, but by accord. If a local maharajah agreed to turn his large land holdings over to the new nation to be divided among his tenant farmers, the nation rewarded him with a large tract of land to keep for himself. He was also allowed to keep all of his personal belongings. The Maharajah of Hyderabad reportedly filled ten freight cars with gold, silver, and precious jewels as he left India.

The Maharajah of Gwalior was rich, not as rich as the Maharajah of Hyderabad, but too rich for me to approve a project for him paid for by American tax dollars. I knew I wouldn't approve his project, but, when he invited me to come to Gwalior, I went. I had never seen such opulence before and I don't think I ever will again.

I flew to Gwalior. A Rolls Royce picked me up at the airport. The maharajah put a Jeep at my disposal for my three-day stay so I could drive around and check out his prospective project. His aide showed me to my own large guest house, complete with a fully stocked refrigerator just in case I got hungry in the middle of the night. The maharajah owned a herd of trained elephants that he used for hunting wild game. He invited me to hunt tiger with him. I had heard of elephant hunting parties, but turned down his invitation. I was not there to shoot animals but to work.

The maharajah invited me to join him for dinner the first evening in his massive dining room. The table was huge, big enough to seat fifty or sixty people. A toy train traveled on a little track on the tabletop carrying assorted condiments from place to place. Buttons at each seat sent the train in either direction. You didn't have to say, "Please pass the curry powder." All you had to do was push a button.

The maharajah was a very nice man, probably in his early forties. I turned down his request for help not only because he could afford it himself, but because what he wanted was too big for an AID demonstration project. However, I did design a project and left it for him to build on his own.

One of the strangest requests for a project had to do with the Russians. The Indians bought all their steel from Britain; the British had a monopoly. The British mined iron ore in India, shipped it back to England for smelting, and then sold the steel to the Indians at a good price. The Indians wanted to make their own steel and needed a mill. They wanted to build it in Bhilai, a village near Raipur.

Why Bhilai? Because there was a small, fiery red mountain near Bhilai filled with iron ore. The Indian government first approached Washington for help in building a steel mill. Washington said no. So the Indians went to Moscow for help.

The Russians said yes. The only problem was that there was no water supply in Bhilai.

Governor Shukla called me into his office. He told me about the project and how badly India needed the steel mill to expand its economy. He said the Russians were eager to build it, but couldn't begin without a water supply. I was building a small earthen dam not too far from Bhilai for a local irrigation project, and he wanted me to make that supply available to the Russians. I told the governor that this was not a decision I could make, but that I would check with New Delhi.

I flew to New Delhi since I couldn't discuss Russian steel mills by telephone. I told my tale to Ambassador Bowles's assistant, and he set up a meeting with the ambassador. I told the ambassador what Governor Shukla wanted, and the ambassador asked me just one question: "Is water more valuable for steel production or for irrigation?" My obvious answer was steel.

Bowles rang a bell and asked the American economist attached to the embassy to hear my story. The economist agreed that water for steel was more valuable. There was no question that economically the Indians needed a steel mill and the Russians needed a water supply if they were to build it. So despite the fact that the U.S. approved and paid for the materials used in the irrigation project, I diverted the water to Bhilai, where the Russians built the steel mill for the Indians.

Nehru wanted big projects. I really didn't want to work on big projects, but for the first three years I was the only civil engineer among the AID technical advisors. I had a request from the Indian government to look at the Narmada River and find a suitable place for a dam. For one trip the government provided a small boat and crew of four who floated and rowed me about ten miles downriver through the magnificent Marble Rock Gorge.

The Narmada River (also known as the Narbada or Nerbudda) is one of the seven sacred rivers of India, second only to the Ganges. Many groups of Hindu temples and cremation *ghats* line its banks. According to one Indian legend, the Narmada River sprang from the body of the god Shiva himself. A Hindu proverb says, "As wood is cut with a saw, so at the sight of the holy Narmada do a man's sins fall away." Some local people considered the Narmada River to be even more holy than the River Ganges and say that Ganga herself, goddess of the Ganges, must dip in the Narmada once a year. Ganga comes to the Narmada in the form of a coal-black cow and returns home pure white, free from all sins. During Pradaksina, a major religious holiday pilgrimage, hundreds of the devout walk sixteen hundred miles up one bank of the Narmada and sixteen hundred miles back down the other.

The banks of the Narmada are lined with village after village. I recommended against building a dam there, knowing how many people would be displaced if the river were dammed. And if such a dam collapsed, hundreds of thousands of people might be killed. But Nehru wanted it. He said, "Don't you have big dams in the United States?" When I said yes, he continued, "Why can't India have big dams, too?" I had no answer. The dam on the Narmada was approved in New Delhi. I don't know if it was ever built.

I worked on only one big dam project during my years in India. I designed the spillway for the Rihand Dam. A spillway is what protects a dam from failure. When the water level behind a dam becomes too high, the excess water must flow safely down the spillway. I was familiar with big dams and spillways because when I was at Colorado A & M, we made model studies for two huge dams built in India, the Bakra and Hirakud. The Bakra, when it was completed in 1954, was then the second largest dam in the world.

The rains were extremely heavy in 1953 following the two prior years of drought, and a dam in northwest India failed at the same time the Indian government was designing a new dam on the Rihand River. Thousands of Indians were killed as floodwaters rushed through their villages. The dam failed because the capacity of its spillway was insufficient. Fortunately, someone in an office in New Delhi noticed that the same men who designed the spillway for the failed dam were designing the spillway for the new one. They wanted a second opinion and went to Ambassador Bowles for help. Bowles went to AID chief Parker, who came to me, the only civil engineer around.

I visited the site of the proposed Rihand Dam and looked out over the valley. I saw village after village below. I shuddered to think of what would happen if this dam failed. I knew I had a challenge before me.

Spillway design is critical to the stability of a dam. If water flows over the top of an earthen dam, it crumbles like butter. Large concrete dams fail not because the volume of water behind the dams creates too much pressure, but because the spillway is underdesigned. The purpose of a spillway is to pass floodwaters safely and decrease turbulence at the toe, or base, of the dam. Turbulence created by falling water at the toe of a dam causes erosion and undercuts the dam until it collapses. If the volume capacity of the spillway is too small, water doesn't just flow over the top of the dam, but arches over it, then drops straight down into the river below, creating massive turbulence.

A spillway must be designed so that the water coming over the top stays on the surface of the spillway. If the volume of water over the face of the spillway is too great, it causes cavitation, which results in serious scarring of the spillway surface. Once cavitation occurs, even though the spillway is repaired, any sizeable flow causes further damage to the repaired areas, possibly leading to dam failure.

The men designing the spillway weren't civil engineers. They knew nothing of water flow and dams. They were statistical mathematicians who went by the book, using fourteen empirical equations to design the spillway. The equations they used to compute their results had been developed by American and British engineering firms for dams built in northeast India.

You can't do that. You can't use the same equations developed for one dam to properly design a spillway for another. Every watershed is different. Since the drainage is different and the runoff is different, the design must be different. The design can't be based on equations using only the size of the catchment area and perhaps the intensities of rainfall.

Results using those fourteen different empirical equations varied from 125,000 cubic feet per second (cfs) to over 700,000 cfs. The statisticians averaged out their results and were going to build a spillway that would carry a maximum of 400,000 cfs.

After looking at almost four hundred years of rainfall data for different parts of India, I decided that a spillway capacity of 400,000 cfs was not nearly big enough. With so many people endangered, it was better to be safe than sorry. I designed the Rihand spillway, to handle 660,000 cfs. My design provided that even if 800,000 cfs came over the spillway, cavitation would occur on the spillway, but the dam itself would not fail. I designed a pattern of blocks for the apron below to decrease the turbulence of the water as it came down the spillway.

An Indian government economist from New Delhi looked at my plans. He couldn't understand why I designed the spillway to pass so much flow. Any increase in the size of the spillway meant the dam had to be higher, which meant the base of the dam must be thicker, substantially adding to the cost of building. I told him the larger spillway was essential to protect the people in the villages below. The economist went back to the minister of development in New Delhi and told him that Resnick was crazy and that the dam would cost far more than they had estimated. But the development minister said Resnick is the boss on this one. Do it. They did.

The spillway was built to handle 660,000 cfs of flow. It wasn't long after I returned to the United States that the Rihand catchment area received extremely heavy rainfall and

the river flooded. I called the manager of the Rihand Dam
Project to find out how the dam and spillway had handled the
rains and flooded river. He was happy to report that the dam
held. The flow over the spillway measured over 440,000 cfs.
I slept easily that night.

Chapter 10

The Caste System
Being Untouchable

Sol teaching a Brahman.

Even though the caste system had been outlawed at the creation of the new Indian nation in 1948, it was alive and well in India in the fifties. One of the first things Governor Shukla told us when we came to Madhya Pradesh was that the caste system was illegal and that if anyone tried to use it, they were subject to legal action.

There were four traditional castes in India: the Brahmans, or priests; Kshatriayas, or warriors; Vaishayas, or merchants and farmers; and Sudras, or servants and laborers. All the castes were born from the body of Brahma: the Brahmans from his mouth, the Kshatriayas from his arms, the Vaishayas from his thighs, and the Sudras from his feet. And then there were the Untouchables, lower than the lowest. All non-Hindus, including Americans, fell into this category.

But caste in India went way beyond these divisions. Every Hindu is born into a caste, and his caste determines his social position throughout his life. There were hundreds of castes, which were then divided into subcastes. The members of each caste had a common occupation. There were weavers of cotton, weavers of silk, fishermen, cotton cleaners, cooks, herdsmen, goldsmiths, tanners, carpenters, blacksmiths, miners, water carriers, hunters, potters, oil pressers, salt makers, and the list goes on and on. Members of a caste form a community, and can marry only among themselves. They can eat only with their own caste members.

On one trip to Raipur to check out the ownership of a parcel of land, I took along an Indian engineer, a Brahman. Most of the engineer trainees were Brahman, since in those days they were the only people who could afford a professional education. As I drove, we passed a poorly dressed Indian farmer, obviously on his way to market, bent almost double under the weight of a heavy bag of rice. I stopped the Jeep and the engineer asked me why I stopped. I told him I was going to give the man a ride into town. He looked at me quizzically and said, "You haven't been in this country very long, have you?"

I said, "You're right. I haven't been here long," and motioned the farmer over to the Jeep.

The Brahman engineer warned me, "This isn't the way things are done in India."

I told him that this was the way things were done in the United States and that he had two choices. He could ride along with the farmer and me or he could walk into town. The Brahman had to get out of the Jeep to let the farmer and his load into the back seat. For a minute or so, I didn't know what his decision was going to be. Would he stick to his principles and not ride with a low-caste person, or would he get back in? It was a hot day and we were still a long way from town. He got back in and rode.

One day a man from a wealthy Brahman family whose land bordered the project I was working on called to invite me to a wedding. I knew it wasn't really me he wanted when he asked if I could bring along Ambassador Bowles. I called Bowles's office and talked to his secretary, telling him that we were all invited to the wedding. The ambassador wanted to know if his attendance was really necessary. I said I thought it was a good idea to maintain good will in the area with the big landowners. Since Bowles intended to visit some missions and speak at the University of Nagpur around the time of the wedding, he agreed to attend. The wedding proved to be quite an experience, as the family was not the typical hospitable Indian family.

When the ambassador, his secretary, his pilot, and I arrived at the door, a brother of the groom warmly greeted us. We left our shoes outside as was the custom and went in for the wedding ceremony. I don't know which part of the ceremony we observed, for Hindu weddings are a thing unto themselves, lasting for three to four days.

I could smell food cooking and soon realized it was time to eat. I knew we should have excused ourselves and left immediately because Brahmans never eat with lower castes. We were not only non-Brahman, but, as Americans, we were on a par with the Untouchables. A family member led our small group to the rear of the house and out into the backyard. As he went back into the house, we heard the door lock behind him.

Our dinner was waiting there for us, spread out on bamboo mats laid on the ground. Our plates were large banana leaves. There were no forks or spoons. There were curries and vegetables and a plate piled high with rice dotted with raisins. At least I thought they were raisins, until they flew away. The yard was a typical Indian backyard, home to pigs, chickens, and other livestock, and, as it was the monsoon season, muddy, very muddy. We looked at each other. We pounded on the door to get back into the house. No one answered. Without a word we climbed over the fence, walked around to the front of the home, threw away our socks, picked up our shoes, and departed. This incident was in stark contrast to the typical generous and hospitable nature of the Indian people.

The next day, Ambassador Bowles was the guest speaker at the opening-day ceremony for the new semester at the University of Nagpur. A large group of state and city officials, faculty, and students turned out to hear him. After he gave his speech, one of the Brahman students raised his hand to ask the ambassador a question.

"Ambassador Bowles," he asked, "Why do you Americans criticize us? Look at the way you treat the Negroes in your country. They are second-class citizens. How do you have the nerve to criticize what we do?"

You could see the color red rise up Ambassador Bowles's face like mercury in a thermometer. His anger was visible. He answered, "You're completely right. We obviously have discrimination against the Negroes in our country. It's hard to change people's opinions and minds. And we're doing a little better."

He continued, "But let me tell you what happened to me yesterday…," and he told them the story of the wedding. When the ambassador finished, he got a standing ovation. The Brahman student sank low in his seat.

If you were a Brahman or other high caste, you could afford an education. Students had to pay for grammar school, but a high school education was free. Things were different for lower-caste children. Sidasio had two bright sons, about eight and nine years old. When I arrived in Nagpur, it was summer, and his boys were always out with the other servants' children playing soccer or cricket at the CP Club. Fall came and school started. His boys were still out there playing ball. I asked Sidasio, "When does school start?" Sidasio said, "It already has." When I asked why the boys were not in school, he said there were no schools for them. When they got bigger, they would become cooks like him.

What a waste! There were many private grammar schools in Nagpur, some very fancy and expensive, and some much more modest. I went to the people in my office and made a survey of which schools were good and yet still had reasonable tuition. Almost everyone agreed that there was one moderately priced excellent school. I decided that was the one I wanted.

I called the school and the secretary answered. I introduced myself and said I was an American advisor working with the Madhya Pradesh government and I wanted to enroll two boys in the school. She assumed they were my children and was ecstatic. The school would gain such prestige having two American boys enrolled. She must have run to tell the headmaster that I had called, for he called me back in minutes to schedule an appointment so I could see the school. I collected Sidasio and the boys and we were off.

The moment the four of us walked into the office, the secretary realized that I didn't mean my sons. Her welcoming smile faded. She hurried in to see the headmaster and told him that I was there with two Indian boys, not only Indians, but sons of a servant. She came back and told me the headmaster wanted to see me alone. Sidasio and the boys were to wait outside.

First, as was normal in Indian society, the headmaster and I had coffee and made small talk. He greeted me with, "Good of you to come," and asked how my work was going. I described some of my work to him. Then it was time to get down to business. He said, "I think those two boys will have a lot of difficulty in my school. I think there would be trouble between the sons of a servant and my other students."

I told him I didn't want to cause any trouble in the school and, if the boys became a problem, I would take them out immediately. He continued, "You know they are different from the other boys in the school." I asked in what way? He hemmed and hawed and finally said, "The boys in my school come from a higher echelon in our society."

I told the headmaster what Governor Shukla told us about the caste system. I told him that if he didn't give these boys a chance, I'd go to the governor and tell him what happened at the school. Of course, he enrolled them, but he still tried to discourage me. He told me that besides tuition, they needed uniforms and books. I replied that I wouldn't put them in school without the proper things to wear and all the books they needed. The headmaster knew when he had lost and enrolled the boys. I took them to my local tailor who made their uniforms, and they were in school.

The boys were very bright, straight-A students. But what was most important to the school was their athletic ability. With their years of practice at the CP Club in soccer and cricket, they were experts. The older boy became captain of the soccer team, and the younger captained the cricket squad. For three years in a row, the school won the soccer and cricket championships in the Nagpur school league.

The school term was six years and I left Nagpur before the boys finished. Before I left, I visited the headmaster to tell him that I wanted the boys to finish and that I would pay for their sixth year. He laughed. He said if he kicked them out after I left, the entire student body would revolt. The boys finished their education. After they graduated, I got them jobs in Ruby's father's huge textile factory. The boy who started in the office became the head office manager. The other worked his way up to became the head floor manager. So much for the Indian caste system.

Chapter 11

Living with Wildlife
Tigers, Snakes, and Other Scary Things

Mary Bell holding Tige and his sisters.

Ronald Noronha's reputation as a tiger killer endeared him to the tribals and won him status among the Gonds. When Noronha arrived in Bastar as district commissioner in 1949, the people weren't impressed with this government official. It wasn't until he shot a tiger who had killed three local farmers that he earned their respect. Noronha told me man-eating tigers kill nearly three hundred villagers a year. I arrived at a local village one day in time to watch him kill another, a white Bengal female who had stayed around the village to care for her three young cubs that were too young to move. Noronha was going to kill the cubs, too, but I volunteered to take the three orphans back to the Nagpur zoo.

The cubs weren't weaned yet. To feed them, I dipped a piece of cloth in a bowl of milk and they sucked on it. One of the cubs, the little male, trailed after me all that day and crawled into my lap whenever I sat down. The next morning I put the three cubs into a cardboard box and loaded them into the back seat of my Jeep for the drive back to Nagpur. It was cold outside, and the little male cub crawled out of the box and into my lap again and again. Each time I returned him to the box. I reached Nagpur too late to take the cubs to the zoo that night, so they stayed with me, and, of course, the little cub found his way into my lap and helped me write my reports. I awoke the next morning to find him curled up on the end of my bed. How could I turn the little fellow over to the zoo?

I dropped two cubs off at the zoo and Tige took up residence with me. He was a fine pet. A Doberman lived in the bungalow next door and each morning Tige bounced up to the fence to say a friendly hello. The Doberman barked ferociously and clawed the fence trying to get to Tige. As Tige grew bigger and bigger, the Doberman's barking and clawing became less ferocious. Eventually, whenever Tige approached the fence, the Doberman backed away and slunk off, tail between his legs.

Tige accompanied me on trips into town in my Jeep, sitting tall in the passenger seat. I'd leave him in the Jeep while I ran my errands, sure that he would draw a crowd and that no one would attempt to steal anything while he was on watch. He growled and snarled at the crowd that gathered to see the tiger in the Jeep. The hair on his back stood on end. As soon as I climbed back in the Jeep, he curled up and fell asleep, his sentry duties over.

At night I walked over to the club for dinner with Tige following closely behind. As we reached the front steps, Tige circled to the back door for his dinner. He'd put his little head through the beaded glass curtain on the kitchen door and growl gently to tell the kitchen staff to fix him a plate. And what a plate it was. No leftovers for Tige. The staff fed him the best there was. After dinner, Tige circled back and lay down at the front steps to wait for me. We walked home together.

Tige's favorite game was "Attack Sol." I'd lie down on the floor while he climbed up on the couch. As a young cub, this was a major effort for him. Then he'd crouch, growl, and launch himself onto my chest. I'd catch him and toss him back onto the couch. Of course, as Tige grew, the game became much easier for Tige. For me, it became much harder.

One night, when Tige was about four months old, I stayed out late and I guess I had a little too much to drink. I went to bed and fell into a very deep sleep. I had closed the door to the bungalow when I came home and Tige needed to go outside. He tried to wake me but I was really out. Claws extended, he raked the side of my face with his paw. I woke up to find Tige licking off the blood. It was time to deliver Tige to the zoo.

The zoo was on my route between home and the office,

and so whenever I was home in Nagpur, I'd stop to visit Tige on the way to work. He'd bound up to the bars, wagging not only his tail but his whole body. I didn't know if he was more interested in seeing me or enjoying the bag of goodies I'd hand feed him for breakfast. The food at the zoo didn't come anywhere near the standards of the club food to which he was accustomed. After returning from a two-month leave in the States, I picked up a bag of food for him from the cooks in the dining room and stopped off at the zoo. I was amazed at how he had grown. Though I was sure Tige recognized me, the zookeeper strongly advised me not to feed him by hand any more. It didn't take me long to decide that he was right.

Central India, especially the Bastar District, was a prime *shikar*, or hunting area, attracting hunters from all over the world who wanted to bag their white Bengal tigers. Tiger hunting is usually done from *charpoys*, rope cots, suspended in trees. But not by Ronald Noronha. He stalked his tigers on foot and shot them from the ground.

I hunted once with Noronha after a group of villagers asked him to kill a tiger that had killed a man in their village. The only time Noronha ever killed a tiger was if it was a proven man-eater.

Noronha carried his big-caliber, double-barreled rifle. His dog, a bull terrier who went everywhere with him, was at his heels. I followed closely behind. Noronha, in a crouch, walked silently up the *nalla*, the dry riverbed where the tiger had last been spotted. As hard as I tried to be quiet, I made all kinds of noises. Noronha turned back to look at me and, if looks could kill, I'd be dead. I tried even harder to move silently.

It wasn't long before the tiger snarled from the riverbank above and then launched himself over the edge of the riverbank straight at Noronha, about twelve or fifteen feet away. Noronha, rifle ready, shot the first barrel. The tiger hit the ground about six feet away. The first shot was not fatal and the tiger kept on coming. Then the dog jumped into the action and prevented the tiger from attacking Noronha. The tiger was confused, stunned to be attacked by the dog. Noronha fired his second barrel and the tiger was dead. I have never been so scared in my life. So scared that I have to admit I wet my pants.

Tigers grow to be very large. Very, very large. I was out one day in a demonstration area with an Indian engineer looking at a possible irrigation project. It had been raining for several days and the sun was finally out. We walked along a wide forest path. I was in front. We came around a bend, and there in front of us, sprawled across the entire path, was a tiger asleep in the sun. I stopped dead. My companion bumped into me and on tiptoes peered over my shoulder and whispered, "Don't move." Don't move? I couldn't have moved if I tried. My feet were deeply rooted to the ground. I felt my companion shaking behind me.

The tiger lazily lifted his huge head and looked at me. He yawned. His canines had to be at least three inches long. He yawned again, stretched out to his full length of more than six feet, and slowly rose to his feet. He looked at me again, turned, and walked into the forest. We had planned to return by way of the same path but found another. I wasn't about to disturb his nap a second time.

Later Noronha explained this event in the way that Indians teach, through storytelling. He told a story about three boys he had met on a forest trail. The two with short hair were schoolboys. The one with long hair was not. He questioned them: "If you saw a tiger staring at you at the next turn of the trail, what would you do?"

The first schoolboy said, "I'd run."

"You're dead," Noronha replied. "No man can run from a tiger."

The second schoolboy said, "I'd climb a tree."

"You're dead, too. A tiger can jump faster than you can climb."

The third boy said, "I'd just stand facing him, and after a while the tiger would go away."

The third boy was right. Noronha explained, "A tiger generally sees you before you see him. He kills from behind. If a man falls face up, the tiger won't eat him. So if you see a tiger standing there looking at you, he isn't going to kill you. If you don't startle him, he will go about his business." I was lucky that I had been too scared to move.

I was with Noronha one day when a group of villagers asked for his help in killing a leopard that had killed a man in their village. He stalked and killed the leopard and asked me if I wanted the skin. Thinking of my sister, I said sure. Over the next few years, he killed many leopards and collected four more skins, perfectly matched for color and spots. I took them home for my sister to make a leopard-skin coat. The furrier had never seen skins like those. Though he had enough skins to make a full coat, he only made her a short

District Commissioner Noronha and a dead leopard.

jacket. For months afterwards, he advertised leopard-skin hats, muffs, and stoles for sale.

Another dangerous animal is the wild buffalo, one of the meanest animals around. They are fast and can be deadly. I avoided the wild buffalo that roamed the Bastar district. The buffalo liked the feed in the village pastures and often mixed in with the domestic bullock herds. The tribal villagers called on Noronha for help in getting them out. Wild buffalo have notoriously poor eyesight, but do have an incredibly good sense of hearing and an even better sense of smell. If they smelled anything unusual, they killed it to protect themselves. I saw the buffalo but made sure they didn't see me. I kept out of their way.

The horns on a wild buffalo can have a twelve-foot spread that prevents them from moving easily through the forest.

When I was out in the field checking out catchments, I made sure to stay clear of open areas. I wouldn't cross an open space. I'd stay near the trees and walk carefully around. It didn't matter that I had farther to go. It was better to be safe than sorry.

Outside of a few ducks for dinner, the only animal I shot in India was a hyena. I was working in the tribal area and sleeping in a tent. Harilal and Sidasio built the fire up at night to keep the wildlife away. I looked out one night and saw two bright, bloodshot eyes, red hyena eyes reflecting the fire-light. Bloodshot hyena eyes are very distinctive, not like the eyes of any other animal.

The hyena stared at my tent. I didn't like it. I wondered if he was trying to decide if I was too big for his dinner. The next night, the hyena not only hung around, but grew a little friendlier and even nosed around inside our campsite. I borrowed a rifle from Noronha and the very next night aimed right between those red, bloodshot eyes. I found the dead hyena the next morning, with one shot between the eyes.

Some wild animals were domesticated. We used elephants to haul the trees we cut down in the forest on the site of a future reservoir. A large, male bull elephant ruled the herd and demanded his right to be first in line and lead the rest of the herd. One female elephant had a young, spoiled baby. Curious, he insisted on being in the center of things, and continuously got in everyone's way.

I decided to put the baby elephant to work and had a tiny harness made for him so he could haul small logs. It worked out really well. The baby tossed his head as he proudly led the pack. I rewarded him with peanuts. I kept the peanuts in my pocket, and whenever he saw me arrive at the project, he ran up to me and searched my pockets with his small trunk until he found his peanuts. Then he ambled over to his mother, and you could hear their stomachs rumble as he "told" his mother all about this nice man who brought him peanuts.

Each elephant has its own *mahout,* or handler, and won't obey anyone else. To climb up on an elephant, a *mahout* takes his sharp stick and taps the elephant on its knee. The elephant bends its front knees to allow the *mahout* to climb up. Elephants only allow their own *mahout* to climb up on their heads. One day I leaned against the little one's mother, and must have touched her knee. She immediately bent her knees and waited for me to climb up. Not to disappoint her, I grabbed her hair in one hand, her ear in the other, and climbed up on her knee. Try as I could, I couldn't hoist myself the rest of the way up. Finally, realizing that I couldn't do it alone, she boosted me up with her trunk. Her *mahout* was astonished. She must have done it because of the kindness I had shown her calf.

And then there were the snakes. India is cobra country. I saw my first cobra when Noronha invited me to see the tribal area for myself. It was a long Jeep trip down to the Bastar district. I arrived at Noronha's house at dusk, just as Noronha, his wife, and their two sons were sitting down to dinner. Their multiroom house, typical of better village homes, had a thatched roof supported by rafters. Lanterns hung on the rafters provided the only light.

As I ate, I sensed a movement in the rafters above my head, but try as I could in the dim light, I wasn't quick enough to see what it was. I sensed it again. Then I saw it! A cobra had wound itself along one of the rafters, and it was his swinging head that caught my eye. I screamed, "Cobra, cobra!" Noronha's kids, trained to show no emotion, began to laugh. Even Noronha and his wife couldn't keep a straight face. The cobra was the family pet and protector. I could not believe my eyes the next morning as I watched the "house cobra" running back and forth with the children as they played soccer.

Why did they need a cobra as protection? The cobra is the natural enemy of another poisonous snake, the beautiful banded krait. Noronha sent me to bed with a flashlight and my first lesson about kraits. Kraits are extremely deadly. If a tribal man is bitten on a finger, he will immediately cut off his own finger so that the poison doesn't spread and kill him. Kraits like warmth and will, if given the chance, crawl in with you and snuggle up along your back. They're not too happy if you turn over on them. They will bite. He also warned me to be extremely careful where I put my feet if I got out of bed at night to use the bathroom, not only because of kraits, but because of the cobra. I was a stranger and he might not like it if I stepped on him. I spent many more nights at Noronha's. Needless to say, I never got up at night.

Not all cobras are pets. The king cobra can reach a length of eighteen feet. Normally a cobra will leave if it hears you coming, but not always. I was near a village one day checking on the irrigation of some rice fields. Rice is grown in paddies surrounded by low earthen mounds built to hold water in the paddies. The rice was almost ripe, but the paddies were still wet. I was walking along the top of an earthen mound when a huge cobra head began to rise up and sway in front of me. The cobra unfurled its hood and I didn't stay around to see much more. As I turned to run, one foot slipped down into the mud of the paddy, and my boot caught. I didn't even notice that my foot had come out until I got back to my Jeep and found I was wearing only one boot. I didn't go back to get it.

Cobra venom is very quick. I was leaving a project one evening to return to Nagpur when one of the Indian engineers told me his wife, who was very pregnant, needed to go into the city. I offered them a ride. As we drove along, I could hear his wife telling him that she needed to make a bathroom stop. He told her to wait. She told him again and again, but he said we couldn't stop. I interrupted and suggested that we stop and she go off into a nearby rice field.

As Indians are extremely modest, she walked quite a ways along the earthen mound surrounding the paddy before she found a place. Unfortunately, that place was close to a cobra's nest and, when she squatted, the cobra bit her repeatedly on the buttocks. She screamed and screamed as we rushed to help her. Our small snakebite kit was useless and she did not survive the attack.

We were always alert for cobras when we were out in the field. Some of the old British circuit houses, while preferable to a tent, were in poor repair, with broken windows and doors. Harilal and Sidasio went to work whenever we arrived at a circuit house. They armed themselves with large sticks and went through the house room by room to make sure there weren't any cobras lurking. They were very unhappy if they found only one, because cobras travel in pairs and they then had to look for a second snake. It is said in India that if you kill a cobra, its mate won't rest until it has revenge. Harilal and Sidasio must have believed the saying. If they didn't find a second snake, we moved on and they pitched my tent.

Cobras and kraits were not the only snakes in India. The royal python of southeastern Asia commonly grows to a length of twenty feet or more. Even though pythons are not poisonous, they are still dangerous. Constrictors, they'll squeeze you to death. Since pythons didn't just live out in the wilds, Sidasio and Harilal went on snake patrol every morning. Four times in the years I lived in India, they found a python curled up on my porch in Nagpur. I knew they had found a snake when I heard them yelling and recognized the chopping noises they made as they hacked up the unwanted visitor. They skinned one of the pythons, and I sent the skin back home to my sister, who had it turned into a purse and pair of shoes to go with her leopard-skin jacket.

Chapter 12

In Sickness and in Health
Dysentery, Cholera, and Leprosy

*The AID public health advisor checking out
Sol's two-squatter.*

I t wasn't easy to stay healthy in India. I had typhoid shots,
cholera shots, yellow fever shots, shots for diseases that
I had never heard of, and took my malaria pills religiously.

Sicknesses of all kinds were endemic in India. One
morning I drove myself to the train depot in Nagpur to pick
up a package and saw a man hanging around there who
seemed almost dead on his feet. He was filthy and covered
with thousands of flies. He was so far gone, he couldn't even

straighten up.

I picked up my package and helped him into the back seat of my Jeep. I don't think he had bathed in more than a year, and I sat him in the corner farthest from me because of the stench. I drove him directly to Dr. Abraham's office. The doctor and his nurses were horrified by what I had done but took him in. They shot him full of antibiotics and checked him into the hospital. The hospital staff stripped him, burned all his clothing, and all but submerged him in a bathtub. I visited him in the hospital and, miraculously, he got better. The hospital outfitted him with new clothing and Dr. Abraham gave him a job cleaning up the clinic. He was eternally grateful to them and to me. He worked hard, long hours and was so anxious to please that sometimes Dr. Abraham or his nurses had to insist that he go home at night.

It was almost impossible to avoid amoebic dysentery, and I didn't. Amoebic dysentery is common in India where human feces are used for fertilizing vegetables and foods are washed in polluted water. It wasn't Sidasio's fault that I got sick. Sidasio boiled all my drinking water for twenty minutes. If I was invited out for dinner at a place with which he wasn't familiar, he'd go over early in the day to inspect the kitchen and check what was on the menu. If he thought there was something I shouldn't eat, he'd tell the servants there that his *Sab* had to be very careful about what he ate and drank and that he, Sidasio, would bring boiled water and cooked food from home for them to serve to me. When the servants came in carefully holding a special plate for me, I knew Sidasio had been there. He didn't want to get fired. He did his job well.

I avoided all uncooked food and stayed healthy until I was invited to attend a meeting in Simla, a hill station in the northern mountains. Naturally, I was going to bring Sidasio and Harilal with me but was told there was no room for servants. Sidasio begged to come along. He pleaded, "Who is going to take care of you, *Sab*?" He told me he didn't need a room but would sleep outside in the Jeep. I left him home anyway. That was my big mistake. Something I ate in Simla caused my case of amoebic dysentery. At that time, there was no cure for the disease, and it plagued me for years until a doctor in Brazil treated it with an experimental drug that worked. As Sidasio nursed me, he moaned that I was going to blame him. I finally convinced him that it wasn't his fault, that his job was safe.

When a smallpox epidemic broke out in one of the northeastern villages of Madhya Pradesh, the state health officer called me to ask if I was going to be driving out anywhere in the affected area. If I was, he wanted to hitch a ride to take vaccine to the local clinic. Since there was no train transportation to the area and he didn't have a state car, it was me or the bus. I said I didn't need to go, but would be happy to make the trip. I picked him up and we headed toward the affected village on small dirt roads.

On the ride up, I asked about the smallpox epidemic. I told him that I thought smallpox had been eradicated throughout the world with vaccinations. He hemmed and hawed, and his face got a little red.

He finally said, "Well, apparently it hasn't been eradicated everywhere in the world." Then he added, "But you

know, Sol, India has problems. We have a huge population.
We have economic problems and it's hard to get money even
for vaccinations. There is no transportation to many of our
small villages. We inoculate many people in the big cities, but
it's hard to reach the people in all the small cities and little
villages."

There were frequent outbreaks of cholera in India. When
it broke out in one of the villages in my demonstration area,
the villagers died like flies. About five hundred of the thousand villagers died in just a week. I telephoned the public
health doctor on our AID team, and he came down from
Delhi on the next flight. We tested the river water that fed
the village pond and found a wasteland of cholera bacteria.
He told the people they were getting sick because they were
drinking polluted water. They didn't believe him. They were
sure the gods were angry. The villagers not only drank the
polluted water, they bathed in it, washed their clothes in it,
and said their prayers in it. The river was sacred to them.
After all, the River Goddess, daughter of Lord Shiva, lived
there. One of the prayers included touching the contaminated river water to their lips. They refused to stop using the
river water.

People don't die from cholera bacteria spread by drinking
water contaminated with human excrement. The cholera bug
causes diarrhea, vomiting, and muscular cramps. The
infected person becomes severely dehydrated. The dehydra-
tion makes the person want to drink more and more water.
All this does is cause more diarrhea, vomiting, and dehydra-
tion until the infected person dies of circulatory collapse or

renal failure. If the infected person drinks only pure water, he or she recovers.

I got in touch with the state engineer who brought down a drilling rig. We dug more wells and, as always, tested the well water. It was pure. When the villagers refused to use the well water, the AID public health doctor had an idea. He assembled all of the villagers for a meeting on the cricket field.

He stood in front of the people and asked, "You know how when your wives menstruate, they are impure? How they cannot cook your food? How you separate them from the rest of the village? How they live alone in their separate little huts when they are impure?" The villagers solemnly nodded yes. He continued, "The same thing happens to the River Goddess. She is menstruating and her water is impure. You cannot use her water to bathe or drink until she is clean again." You could see the light grow in their eyes as they comprehended what he said. They got the message. As they began to use the well water, they found that they actually liked it better than the river water and continued to drink it after the cholera epidemic subsided.

Getting the villagers to drink clean water was enough to stop the cholera epidemic. A bigger problem was to prevent cholera epidemics in the first place. There had to be a way of preventing human excrement from contaminating the water. The villagers didn't have bathrooms. They didn't even have outhouses. Every morning you could see the villagers walk up the road, men moving off to the right, women to the left. It was a social occasion. They squatted with a view of the road so they wouldn't miss a thing.

I designed what euphemistically became known as a two-squatter, and had a series of them built of brick on raised concrete slabs on each side of the road. The only mistake I made was in closing them in on three sides with reed walls for privacy. The villagers refused to use them. The two-squatter had too much privacy and no view of the road. I had the reed walls taken down, but the villagers still preferred their old sites on the side of the road.

It wasn't until the monsoons came again that they realized that not only was there no mud on the slabs, but the view of the road was much better. The villagers made the change. Word got around the AID group about my invention of the brick two-squatter. When I walked into a meeting in Delhi shortly afterwards, my fellow AID advisors, all ninety-five of them, rose and gave me a standing ovation.

The Indian government built medical clinics in the demonstration areas. I was working on a project near a clinic that had a male sterilization program. As usual, when we were living out in the field, Harilal and Sidasio had pitched my tent on a high point to try to avoid the flies. The point overlooked the clinic, and I watched lines of men slowly enter the clinic at one end and exit at the other end, carefully clutching something in their hands. I had no idea what was happening in the middle. I found out when some of the men working on my project asked for time off to go to the clinic for the sterilization procedure. It was a voluntary program, and the men who participated were rewarded with small transistor radios. Of course, I let them go. I was amazed to see that some of the men went two and three times to the clinic and accumulated quite a collection of radios.

In 1952, malaria was still rampant in the countryside of India. Malaria doesn't often kill, but sure makes you miserable, causing fatigue, headaches, and alternating high fever and severe chills. It doesn't go away, just into remission, and can recur many times. In the late 1940s, the Indian government stepped up the fight against malaria, and in 1949, the antimalaria squads arrived in the tribal villages of Bastar. Ronald Noronha told me about the villagers' reactions.

The tribal people wouldn't let the officials take blood samples. After all, they thought, blood is taken only for a sacrifice. And they wouldn't let them spray the white DDT powder on the walls of their houses because this was obviously a form of magic. When the antimalaria workers did spray the houses, the people wiped the DDT from the walls. But as they slowly learned to accept and appreciate medical care, they also realized that if the malaria-carrying mosquitoes were killed, they wouldn't get sick. They could go back to enjoying life, the thing that was most important to them.

Leprosy was another disease that occurred in India. I remember the first time I saw a person with leprosy, about three weeks after I settled into Nagpur. Harilal was driving me back from my first tour of a demonstration area to look at possible project sites, and we were almost home. It was hot, very hot, and I was not yet used to the heat. I don't think I ever got used to the heat.

Harilal stopped for petrol. I got out of the Jeep and leaned against it, in a half daze. I was daydreaming about the cold bottle of beer in my refrigerator in the bungalow when something soft and mushy touched me lightly on the arm. I raised my hand and brushed it off. It happened again, this time a little harder. I looked back and there was what looked like a bag of rags with an arm sticking out. The arm had no hand; it ended at the wrist. It was a leper covered with bandages and he had touched me! I was petrified. I was going to become a leper, too.

We had passed an American Baptist Leprosy Hospital about twenty miles back. All dreams of a cold beer forgotten, I told Harilal we had to go back to the hospital. He saw how frightened I was and drove there as quickly as he could. I ran in and an American nurse greeted me. She asked if she could help me and I blurted out, "I'm Sol Resnick, an American stationed here working with AID. I've just been touched by a leper and I need help."

"Did he touch you on an open cut or sore?" she asked.

"No," I answered. I pointed to my arm and said, "He touched me here, right here. You have to help me."

She began to laugh and said she'd get the doctor to look at my arm. The doctor hurried out of his operating room, stripping off his gloves as he came, leaving his patient on the table. After all, Americans were much more important than Indian patients. He looked at my arm, saw no open cuts, and told me I'd be fine. But I was still worried and pleaded he had to do something. He laughed and told me he'd been working with and operating on lepers for forty years and hadn't caught it yet. But to ease my mind, he had the nurse swipe my arm with some alcohol.

The doctor and I became good friends, and I stopped off

at the mission hospital whenever I was in the area. I tried to be at any American hospital or mission around mealtime because there was usually American food available prepared under somewhat sanitary conditions. On my visits, I noticed that the patients didn't have anything to do but sit around and feel sorry for themselves. I talked to the doctor and suggested that I design an irrigation project so that they could have a garden. I drew up some plans and left them with him.

Nothing happened. There was no garden. The patients still sat around. When I asked why they weren't building the project, the doctor said they had barely enough money to keep the hospital going. There was no money for anything else. I thought for a minute and decided to approve the project as an official AID demonstration project. The U.S. would provide the material and the patients the labor. I felt it was a worthwhile project, but I didn't tell Delhi what I was doing. I was afraid they would say no.

It was a great project. No matter how incapacitated the patients were, they all pitched in and worked. They built the irrigation project and grew their own food. And, because they had work to do, farming their own food and feeling useful, their health improved. Other missionaries heard about the project and came from all over India to see what the hospital had done. They all wanted projects of their own. But I wasn't there for the missionaries. I did what I could on my vacation time and trained people on missionary property, but I kept quiet about it.

Chapter 13

Visitors

Nagpur, the Crossroads of India

U.S. Ambassador Chester Bowles arrives in Nagpur.

Many people came to visit Nagpur during my tour. They came from the Ford Foundation, which was one of the sponsors of the program, and from various universities. There were salesmen from equipment companies such as Caterpillar, Massey Ferguson, and International Harvester. Many U.S. government officials came, including congressmen, senators, and politicians running for office. We were expected to wine and dine them.

One visitor I remember very well was Adlai Stevenson.

Stevenson was different from the rest. He had just lost his first bid for the presidency but still wanted to keep current in foreign affairs. He seemed truly interested in what we were doing for the Indian people. He didn't lecture me about what he thought we should be doing in India. He wanted to learn what I thought.

Stevenson, a good friend of Chester Bowles, stayed with me at the CP Club. We had dinner at the club and came back to the bungalow to have a beer and talk. Stevenson put me at ease. He wanted me to be truthful. He said that when a politician comes out to look at a program, it's difficult for someone who is part of the program to say it's a bad program, since it wouldn't make him or the program look good. Then he asked me if there was any way I thought Washington could improve on the AID program.

I told him how I felt about what we were doing. I told him how lucky we were to have Chester Bowles and Nehru, both brilliant men, administering the program. I told him how we trained twelve to fifteen engineers on each project in irrigation, how we trained large classes in agricultural techniques, how we didn't just give the Indians money, but taught them to provide for themselves. I told him that the United States spent $12 million for the program and that it had done an amazing job. Stevenson agreed that it was money well spent.

Another visitor's reason for coming to Nagpur was more mysterious. The American Embassy in New Delhi had sent an American woman from the State Department on a special assignment to Madhya Pradesh and wanted help from me. I was instructed to pick her up at the airport in Nagpur, find accommodations for her, and set up meetings with Judge Hemeon and some people in Raipur. They didn't tell me any more except that her name was Barbie.

I made the necessary arrangements. I booked rooms for Barbie at the club and called Judge Hemeon. He agreed to meet with her and asked how much time he should set aside. I replied that I had no idea what she wanted to talk about or how long it would take. He said he'd book an appointment for an hour and, if it took longer, he would change his schedule. Everyone else I called said the same thing.

I picked Barbie up at the airport and was delightfully surprised. She was a beautiful, young Jewish woman. I took her to the club where we had dinner, and the next day I drove her to her appointment with the judge and waited to take her back. She thanked him as she left, and he replied, "If Sol asks me to do something, how can I say no?"

The next day I drove her to Raipur and she met with all the people on her list. I still had no idea why she was there. On the third day I reluctantly took her back to the airport. She thanked me for my help and added that she had come out to the desert and found a real gem. She wrote from New Delhi and I wrote back. I spent time with her whenever I went to Delhi. She was transferred to the embassy in London, and I detoured through London on my way back to the States to visit her there. I never did find out why she came to Nagpur.

I was really happy when Mr. Savage, a geohydrologist who had been involved in building the Hoover Dam, arrived in New Delhi as an advisor in 1955. He was supposed to work out in the field, but being over the age of seventy, he found living in a tent a bit too strenuous. AID put him to work in New Delhi. Fortunately for me, he was bored in Delhi and often came down to Nagpur to see what I was doing. He was very helpful in locating sites for wells and taught me a lot about the geology of the region.

Another hydrologist who came to visit in Nagpur was Professor Israelson of Utah State, one of the world's foremost authorities on irrigation. AID had asked him to come out on a short assignment to see what I was doing. They were probably worried because they couldn't understand why I asked Washington to send wheelbarrows and shovels instead of big tractors. Israelson was deaf and traveled with his wife, who interpreted for him. I took them out to see the demonstration areas and was pleased when he approved of my work.

It wasn't just visitors from the States who came to see the demonstration projects. From the very first time my boss, Frank Parker, heard about the tribal villagers in the Bastar District, he wanted to see the villages for himself. He'd tell me, "Sol, I've got a couple of free days, I'd like to come down and see some of your projects." I'd tell him that a couple of days weren't enough. He would have to fly to Nagpur, we'd drive to Raipur, and then drive all day to see the tribal villages. I told him he'd need at least a week.

Finally he said he had a week off and was coming down. He flew into Nagpur and we were off. When we reached Raipur, we turned right onto the local dirt and gravel roads and went south toward the Gondavi River, passing many tribal villages. It was the local market day. People walked to market carrying baskets of vegetables they had grown and fruit and berries they had picked. They carried things they wanted to sell that they had made from animal skins. Young, bare-breasted girls, clad only in their normal, wide, white band of cloth tied low on their hips, carried their wares in woven wicker baskets balanced on their heads. When they walked, their heads were still. All their movement was in their swaying hips. There were two lines of women, one coming, one going. Parker, his eyes glued to the continuing bare-breasted procession, didn't say a word for over two hours. Then he commented, "Now I know why the U.S. is building so many projects in Bastar."

Back in New Delhi, Parker told everyone at the embassy about the tribal women. He told the doctors and nurses at the embassy clinic. Every time I came into the clinic, the nurses teased me about all the work I did in Bastar. They even asked, "If we go topless, will you come in to see us more often?" I think they liked to see me blush.

Not all visitors were so agreeable. It was easy to work with the first comptroller assigned to distribute money to the AID advisors. I'd tell him what I wanted and what I wanted it for, and he gave it to me. He never said no. The second comptroller was another story. He went strictly by the book. If it wasn't in the book, he said no. He insisted that all of our time had to be spent working on our projects, with no time off. I got tired of begging funds for my innovations and bypassed him. I went directly to the ambassador and his assistant and always got what I needed.

But as strict as the new comptroller was with our use of

AID funds, he threw caution to the wind when it came to something for himself. I got a letter from him one day saying he had ten days of vacation and wanted to kill a tiger to take home with him. Would I set it up? He expected me to pick him up at the airport and host him in my quarters at the CP Club. He also expected me to drive him to Raipur. This from the man who had lectured me on going by the book.

I didn't know what to do. I definitely didn't want to spend any time with this man. I called Frank Parker and told him about the letter. Parker said I couldn't say no, but I could try to dissuade him. He suggested I write back to the comptroller saying that I was very sorry, but I could drive an AID vehicle only when I was on official business. Parker told me to reserve a room for the man at the Mount Hotel and, as an aside, describe my own experience there with the roaches. He told me to recommend Governor Shukla's son, a professional hunter, who could take him hunting for a fee. I followed Parker's good advice and gave the comptroller the young hunter's address and telephone number. I never heard from the comptroller again about hunting tigers.

There were other visitors. I hadn't been in India long when I received a call from a man working in Pakistan for the Peter Kewit engineering firm, offering me an engineering job in Pakistan, sight unseen. Sight unseen, I said no. He offered to double my salary if I would come to Pakistan. I still said no. A few days later, he arrived in my office in Nagpur carrying pictures of the walled enclave where Kewit had created a small American city in rural Pakistan. There were beautiful homes with green lawns, schools, a PX for shopping, a golf course, tennis courts, parks, and movie theaters. He couldn't entice me. I still said no. I'm not sorry.

Shortly before I finished my second two-year tour, Dean Harold Meyers, head of the College of Agriculture at the University of Arizona, was invited to the University of Nagpur to upgrade its agriculture curriculum. Parker told me the dean was coming and asked me to pick him up at the airport, find him a room, and help him in any way I could. I took Dean Meyers to the university, but, as was typical of the Indians, they weren't ready for him yet. It was the dry season and I was working as hard as I could. Rather than leave him alone in Nagpur, I took him with me to visit the projects while I worked.

During the dry season in central India, you can ride for a hundred miles in oppressive heat and not see a soul. Then you come to an irrigated area and everything is different. Everything is green, everything is growing, and the villagers are out working, fixing up their houses and their schools. He was impressed. After Meyers met with the University of Nagpur people and laid out a way to improve the curriculum, he went back to Tucson. Little did I know how important that visit would be to the rest of my career.

After nearly five years in India, I left for AID headquarters in Washington, D.C., to spend five months writing a handbook on small irrigation projects for use in other third-world countries. Dean Meyers called me in Washington and offered me the position of director of the University of Arizona's new Institute of Water Utilization. I had many choices. I was asked to stay on at AID headquarters. I was invited to go back to the University of Wisconsin as an associate professor. Stanford, UC Berkeley, MIT, Colorado State, and the University of Utah all offered me faculty positions and the opportunity to finish my Ph.D. But I couldn't resist the opportunity to have a free hand and start a new institute, especially in a desert area where irrigation was so important. When I finished the handbook, I headed west to the University of Arizona in Tucson, a decision I've never regretted. Hopefully, they didn't regret it either. They honored me with an Honorary Doctorate of Science in 1993.

Chapter 14

Travels
Around India and the World

Ferrying across the Narbada.

As the only irrigation engineer among the ninety-six American advisors, I was requested to approve projects all over India and saw much of the country. There were no main roads to many Indian villages. Some of the so-called roads that did exist were little more than cart trails. Traffic on even the paved, main roads was slow, delayed by bullock-drawn carts, horse-drawn tongas, bicycles, overloaded buses, people on foot, and stray cows. Harilal drove very slowly and carefully. I spent a lot of time on those roads and trails.

Driving through the rolling hills east of Raipur one day at sunset, I saw what remains the most beautiful scene in my memory. As we topped the saddle of a hill, I saw terrace after terrace of rice paddy stretching to the valley below before the road climbed back up the next rise. Good paddy rice has white blossoms. Cheap paddy rice is multihued. This was cheap paddy, and the blue, pink, red, yellow, purple, lilac, and red blossoms ruffled by a light breeze formed ever-changing rainbow reflections on the paddy water.

Harilal didn't always drive. Sometimes I went off on my own to scout out a project. I wasn't happy to be alone the day I drove slowly along a forest road studded with tree trunks. As I weaved between the trunks, I spotted a panther loping along in the shade of the forest, his eyes glued to me, easily keeping pace with my open Jeep. There was nowhere for me to turn and, for the next ten miles, we were close companions. Too close. All I could think was, "Am I this guy's lunch?" To my great relief, he finally turned off.

Wild animals weren't the only reason it wasn't good to travel the roads of India at night. Even though most of the circuit houses and guesthouses built by the British were in a sad state of disrepair, it was still better to stop than to push on. One afternoon I took longer at one project than I had planned. We got a late start heading for our next project where we had planned to spend the night. It was early evening, getting dark outside, and we still had miles to go to reach our destination. I was half dozing in the back seat but noticed Harilal drive past a man asleep on a rock on the side of the road. I insisted that Harilal stop and offer him a ride.

Harilal argued that we would be even later, but he finally stopped, turned the Jeep around and went back to pick him up.

The man was not someone who wanted a ride. He was a guard posted by the police to stop every traveler driving through that area at night. The area was under the control of *dacoits*, a group of thieves who robbed and killed anyone who came through. The now wide-awake guard took us to the local guesthouse where we stayed overnight. The next morning, armed guards convoyed all the local travelers safely through the area. Sometimes good deeds pay off.

But sometimes bad things happen to people who deserve better. After I left India, Harilal went to work for an American woman AID advisor who had arrived in Nagpur. He was driving her to a meeting in Bombay, and as they neared the city, there was some roadwork. A detour through small villages was poorly marked. Harilal got lost. He stopped in one of the villages looking for the local schoolteacher to get directions to Bombay.

He stopped in the wrong village. Men in Bombay, Calcutta, and other large cities kidnapped poor village children, maimed them severely by cutting off their limbs or blinding them, and then put them out into the streets to beg for them. This village had recently lost a couple of children to the kidnappers who had been driving an American Jeep. When the village people saw a similar Jeep drive into their village, they pulled the woman from the vehicle and began to beat her and Harilal with sticks and rocks. Fortunately, the schoolteacher heard the commotion, and Harilal was able to tell him the woman was an American AID advisor. She was very badly injured. The schoolteacher helped Harilal drive her to a hospital in Bombay.

Sometimes the only means of transportation to a project was the back of an elephant. It took four days to reach one village south of Calcutta, four days in the monsoon season, crossing flooded rivers. Four days was a long time to sit and sway on the back of an elephant.

I didn't know how smart elephants were until, stiff as a board, I needed to stretch. I stood up and turned to look back at the trail behind us. I didn't see that my elephant was approaching a tree with a low branch, a branch that would have hit me in the head and knocked me to the ground. The elephant stopped in his tracks. The *mahout,* not realizing why the elephant stopped, jabbed at him to get him to move on. The elephant wouldn't move. The *mahout* yelled at the elephant and beat him, but the elephant still refused to budge. I turned forward to see what was going on and saw the branch. I sat down and the elephant swayed off again.

When we'd reach a river, the *mahouts* took everything off the backs of the elephants to let them drink and cool off in the water. One day it was about 118 degrees Fahrenheit and I was hot. While the elephants played in the water, I decided to cool off, too. I walked over to a log on the riverbank, sat, and began to untie my boots so I could wade out to another log in the water and cool my hot feet. I couldn't figure out why people began to shout at me. I didn't understand what they were shouting until the "log" in the river swam off. It was a crocodile.

But it wasn't always possible to get from place to place even on the back of an elephant. Once, my elephant transport dropped me off at a demonstration project planning to come back for me in a few days. But an early, severe monsoon storm arrived and dumped torrents of rain in the rivers. The rivers rose and their currents became so swift that even the elephants couldn't cross. AID sent a plane to fly over the project to make sure I was safe. Because I was there for over a week, I was really happy when they air-dropped food packages.

I avoided flying in and out of Nagpur if I could find another way to travel because the old DC3s flying the internal air routes of India had seen better days. When you made a plane reservation in Nagpur, they sold the seats in the front of the plane first and then worked their way toward the back. Any seats left over were filled with cargo. Not an inch of space was wasted and the planes were usually overloaded.

My fears of flying were confirmed on the day one very overloaded plane crashed into the jungle on takeoff from Nagpur. Everyone aboard was killed. The president of the airline held an inquiry into the crash and determined that the plane crashed not because it was overloaded, but because of pilot error. He wanted to prove he was right and ordered another flight with a similar plane as fully loaded as the first. His brother, a pilot for the airline, flew the test plane. It, too, crashed on takeoff. Fortunately, the second plane was filled with cargo, not people. Only the pilot was killed.

When I didn't fly or drive, I rode the train, traveling first-class to be sure to have a seat. Sometimes more passengers hung from the outside of the second- and third-class cars than sat inside. I'd wonder if they managed to hang on until they got to wherever they were going. At the railroad stations, whole families squatted on the platforms, surrounded by cloth bundles holding all their possessions. Train travel was slow due to frequent stops to take on water for the locomotive. There was no food service on the train, but at each stop you could buy anything on the station platform from a *chapati,* an Indian flat bread, to a sit-down, six-course meal.

I'd board the train in Nagpur at 6:00 A.M. and reach Calcutta about 6:00 P.M. On one trip, the train stopped as usual for thirty to forty minutes in the city of Sambalpur, in the province of Orissa, to take on water and clean up the train before continuing into Calcutta. Food and fruit vendors boarded the train and passed up and down the aisles selling their wares. A young, enterprising salesman boarded there as well, carrying a basket of twelve beautifully hand-painted plaster of paris figurines, each about four inches tall, dressed in native costumes. There was a postman with his mail pouch; a *paniwallah,* a water seller, carrying his waterskin; a turbaned Sikh soldier; a laundryman with his bundle; and a hotel waiter, tray balanced on his upraised arm.

I thought to myself, I'd pay twenty rupees for that set of figurines, about four dollars and twenty cents. He saw my light-skinned face and made a beeline for me, sensing he had his mark for the day.

I said in my most disinterested voice, "How much are they?"

He replied, "Only four rupees, *Sahib.*"

I thought that was a great price. But I was on my way to Calcutta. Why buy them now and have to carry them all over the city? I decided to buy them on my way home. I said, "No thanks."

The train whistle blew. The vendors headed for the exits. The figurine salesman rushed up to me at the last possible second and breathlessly said, "*Sahib, Sahib,* only two rupees." How could I refuse?

I carefully carried my basket off the train in Calcutta where an AID man waited for me. He asked, "Are those what I think they are? Isn't it amazing? For the life of me I can't understand how they can make those little figures and sell them for only one rupee." I still have the figurines.

I'll never forget another trip to Calcutta. AID sent me there to meet a ship from the U.S. filled with equipment on route to all the AID programs in the Far East. It was my job to sort out this equipment and reroute it to its final destinations. Maybe they sent me because I was the only engineer among the advisors and they thought the job needed an engineering mentality. They sent me lists, long lists of the equipment to be organized and reshipped by ship, rail, plane, or truck to destinations in Malaysia, Thailand, Burma, Pakistan, and sites all over India.

It was dark when I checked into my hotel. I pulled the drapes and settled down at a desk to work on my lists. Tired, I fell asleep before I finished. Knowing I still had much planning to do, I awoke between three and four in the morning and went back to the desk. Around five o'clock, I needed to stretch and pulled open the drapes to watch the sunrise. It was still dark. But as the dawn broke, I saw a large park across the street, covered not with grass, but with people. Almost every inch of ground was covered by thousands of homeless sleeping men, women, and children.

As the sky lightened, the women were the first to rise. They took their clay pots and went to outlets on the edge of the park for water. When they returned, they took cow dung and small sticks from their burlap bags and laid small fires to cook breakfast for their families. The children rose next and, finally, the men. I watched as the families squatted around the fires and ate their breakfasts. After the meal, everyone packed up. They rolled their sleeping mats and packed all their meager belongings in burlap bags. There was a general exodus as they left the park. I was mesmerized.

But not quite everyone left the park. Bodies still lay on the ground. As I watched, bullock-drawn carts converged on the park, each cart with a two-man team. The men approached the bodies, one by one checking to see if they were dead or alive. If the body lay face down on the ground, they turned it over with their foot. If the body was face up, they simply kicked it to see if there was any response. If the person was dead, the two men heaved the body onto their cart, piling dead body on top of dead body. When the cart was full, they drove off to the river to empty their loads. I later asked someone if they burned the bodies. They didn't. They just took them to the river and dropped them in.

AID also sent me to work in other countries. I went to Ceylon, now Sri Lanka, to demonstrate cloud seeding. There

I found the U.S. government AID program paying for everything, building large structures with heavy equipment. The individual farmers were not involved. I attended conferences in Pakistan and in Japan.

The Washington AID office sent a man from the Bureau of Reclamation to teach irrigation at a meeting in Ankara, Turkey, but the Turkish government wanted advice on small village irrigation projects, not big dams. AID remembered me in India and sent me to Turkey for a week to teach. It was quite an experience.

The first night there I drank toast after toast of strong *arak,* the Turkish national liquor, and awoke with a large hangover the next morning. Then, instead of coffee breaks, the Turks had beer breaks. I have no recollection of anything I taught that week, but I must have done well, because I received a standing ovation.

India was not all work. I visited many of the basic tourist attractions. Of course, I went to Agra and saw the magnificent Taj Mahal built by Shah Jahan for his beloved Mumtaz. In New Delhi, I visited the Red Fort built of red sandstone by the same Moghul ruler, Shah Jahan, as well as Chnadni Chowk, the huge, crowded market nearby. I saw the magnificent Buddhist carvings in the caves at Ajunta and Ellora, viewed the erotically carved temples of Khajaraho, and watched bodies being burned on the cremation *ghats* beside the Ganges at Benares.

In Bombay, I saw the Towers of Silence where the Parsi place their dead for the vultures to clean the bones. I went out to Elephanta Island and saw the huge carvings of Lord

Shiva. In the cities and along roads, I passed large and small wayside shrines built to Shiva and Ganesh and multiple other gods, covered with bright yellow chrysanthemum petals. I watched as the people prepared the hill town of Dharmsala for the Dalai Lama as he entered exile. I spent one vacation on a houseboat in Kashmir, went to Thailand, visited Angkor Wat in Cambodia, and did a tour of Japan.

On my two-month leave after the first two years in India, I stopped in Israel on the way home. It was a busman's holiday. I was invited to Israel to demonstrate my cloud-seeding technique. After the demonstration, I visited a few Israeli projects. I was curious. After all, this was where I was supposed to be working.

The Israelis were pumping water from the Hula swamp to reclaim the land for farming. I watched as they removed an underground rock ridge. I asked the local Israeli engineer where he was going to get gates to replace the rock they were removing. He answered, "We're not putting in gates, we just want to drain the swamp."

I told him, "You can't do it that way. With gates, you control the flow of the river. To keep the area in condition for farming, you must put in gates to raise and lower the groundwater table. Without gates, the marshy soils will dry out and blow away, and the earth will subside." He asked, "Who invited you?" and told me to go away. When I visited the same site a number of years later, I found the soil had dried out and blown away.

My next stop was to watch the Israelis lay a water pipeline from Lake Kinneret to Mitzpe Ramon in the Negev Desert.

They dug a channel and were laying the pipe directly on the ground instead of on a bed of gravel. I asked the engineer in charge of the project, "Where's the gravel?"

He said, "What gravel?"

I told him, "When the ground gets wet, there are large earth movements, and the pipe will break. If you lay the pipe on a bed of gravel, there will be less movement of the pipe. The pipe becomes more flexible."

He said, "We don't need to use gravel. Get lost."

While in Israel a few years later, I checked it out, and the pipeline did indeed need to be replaced. Getting the feeling that I wasn't wanted in Israel, I continued back home to the U.S. for my leave.

I went home via London. Rather than fly, I decided to cruise home on a large, luxurious passenger ship. I looked forward not only to five days of vacation, but to good food. Everything went well as the ship disembarked. Everything went well until we sailed into an incredible storm. The winds raged through the night, and the waves towered higher and higher. I awoke hungry, fantasizing about just what I would have for breakfast. Would it be bacon and eggs, pancakes, waffles? I dressed and carefully made my way through the heaving ship to the dining room. Not a soul was there. A waiter peeked out through the kitchen door and was astonished to see me. He came to my table and asked what I was doing there.

"I'm here for breakfast," I replied.

"Breakfast?" he asked.

I could see him thinking, how could anyone keep anything

in his stomach on this storm-tossed ship? He gave me a menu and asked me what I wanted to eat. I told him I really couldn't decide, that everything looked good. I told him that I had been in India for two years and looked forward to a real American breakfast.

He went back into the kitchen and gave my order to the cook. He, too, couldn't believe there was anyone on board who wanted to eat. He came out to confirm the waiter's story and then, finally convinced, made me a platter of everything. I truly enjoyed my bacon, eggs, pancakes, and waffles.

When it was time to return to India, my flight schedule took me back from New York via London to Bombay. The flight from New York to London was delayed and I missed my Bombay connection. The Pan Am agent told me not to worry. They had arranged an alternate flight for me. They didn't tell me the route. I didn't ask.

I boarded my new Pan Am flight. In those days, Pan Am planes had some bunks for sleeping. After we were in the air, I asked the flight attendant to make up my bunk and she did. She asked if I wanted to be awakened when we landed in Cairo. Cairo? I didn't want to go to Cairo. Nasser had recently taken over Egypt, and Cairo was not a good place for a nice Jewish boy. I told the flight attendant that I preferred to sleep through our stop in Cairo. She asked for my diplomatic passport so she wouldn't have to wake me later. I went to sleep.

I was still sleeping when we landed. The airport was crawling with Egyptian soldiers. Some of them boarded the plane and loudly called, "Where's Resnick?" They opened the sliding door to my bunk and insisted that I accompany them to the terminal. I argued but finally put on pants and a shirt and went with them. I was led into an interrogation room.

An officer asked, "Why are you in Cairo?"

I replied, "I'm here because you took me off the plane."

Again, "Why did you come here?"

"I didn't come here. I'm on my way to India. I don't want to be here," I answered.

The questioning went on and on in the same vein. I heard an announcement over the terminal loudspeaker that my Pan Am flight was leaving for Bombay. My heart sank. The pilot of my plane came into the room and said he wasn't leaving without me. The Egyptian officers told the pilot he was getting on his plane and taking off. I was sure I was done for. The pilot insisted that he be allowed to call the Swiss Embassy to have an official come to protect me because there was no U.S. Embassy in Cairo at that time. At that point, the Egyptians gave up and told the pilot to take me with him. Breathing a huge sigh of relief, we ran for the plane. As the pilot warmed up the engines, I sat frozen in my seat.

The pilot came back to talk to me after he took off and asked me what all that had been about. I told him the only explanation I could think of was that my passport said I was Jewish and I had visited Israel six weeks before.

As we approached Bombay, we circled the city at about ten thousand feet. I don't know if it was my imagination or if I could actually smell the cow dung fires below. But the burning cow dung smelled like home, and I was happy to be back for my next two-year stint.

Chapter 15

Namaste
Goodbye India

Sol.

In 1957 it was time to say *namaste,* goodbye, to India. It was time to go to work in a real office. I left many projects only partially completed. Generally, I'd lay out a project, begin construction, and leave it for the villagers to complete. For example, if it was a diversion project, I'd supervise concreting the first fifty or so feet of canal and leave enough cement and rebar to finish the job. But I always wondered, did the villagers really finish it? Did they do it right? How did it come out? Do the seals on the dams leak? What happened in the villages when they had water for irrigation? I was able to return to India twice to visit some of the projects and answer my own questions.

The first time I went back was in 1959. I was on my way home to Tucson from Thailand where I had helped set up the engineering department at the new SEATO Graduate School of Engineering outside of Bangkok.

I flew to Nagpur and drove out to see some of the nearby projects. I was pleased. The projects I had begun had been carefully completed and were well maintained. Many of the young engineers I had trained were hard at work. It was wonderful to see the changes our agricultural and irrigation techniques had brought. The villagers were well fed. They had better houses, new schools, and medical clinics.

There is no question that the years I spent in India affected the rest of my life. I used methods developed in India in my work in other third-world countries and used examples from my work in many of my classes. I taught my students how to gather data such as rainfall records, run-off records, efficiency records, and how to measure watershed size. They learned sophisticated methods for applying this data when they designed their own projects.

I maintained contact with many of my Indian friends. Joshi and his wife stopped off in Tucson to visit when they came to the U.S. to visit relatives. Patil and Joshi both sent a steady stream of graduate students to the United States. As head of the Water Resources Research Center at the University of Arizona, I was in contact with my counterparts at Colorado State, Utah State, and the University of

California at Davis. We found funding for many Indian students and sent them back to work in India after they had earned their degrees. India used these highly trained engineers to expand the original thirty-two experimental areas.

I made my last visit to India in 1961, after completing a project for the U.S. State Department in the Philippines. I went back to see one of the small villages in a demonstration project. When I arrived in the village, the head of the *panchayat* greeted me warmly. He took me by the hand and I thought he was going to show me how they had completed their project. Instead, he led me over to the center of the village. All the villagers crowded around us. There, high on a pedestal, stood a crudely carved log statue of a man. The thing that struck me most about the statue was the nose, a nose much bigger than the typical Indian villager's nose. It was a nose, I must admit, that was quite similar to mine.

"That's you, *Sab*," he said. "That's in honor of you."

I don't think I could have received a better reward for my years in India.

Afterword

With a heavy heart, I have been reading recent articles regarding construction of large dams in India to provide water for irrigation.

Indian villages, in which the people are very poor and live on the crops they grow on their one to two acres, are near the fertile river flood plains. Building large dams creates large reservoirs that drown out villages and their farms. Large dams and irrigation canals also require careful and costly maintenance. Otherwise, leaking canals kill the fertile soil alongside with salts. The world, sadly, is full of examples of large dam and canal failures because of poor maintenance.

The development of small village irrigation systems, built and maintained by the villagers, was the aim of the USAID program during my five years in India. Instead of flooding out villages and their farms, the small systems increased the villagers' crop yields, which improved their lives by providing funds for more varieties of food, schools, medical facilities, etc.

I knew there was a strong desire on the part of the Indian government to build large dams. Prime Minister Nehru was convinced that India needed large dams to modernize the country. We talked about it. Nehru believed, as did others in the fifties, that the western United States developed because of the construction of dams. Now we're reading that large dams, including those in the American west, aren't so great. Serious consideration is being given to removing dams and restoring rivers to their original condition for the benefit of fish and wetlands.

Because of Nehru's interests, I was not surprised when the Indian government sent me to look at the Narmada River in central India for possible large dam sites. There were many sites, but I strongly recommended against construction because of the inevitable flooding out of hundreds of villages. I strongly recommended in favor of the continued training of engineers to develop small village irrigation systems.

To my dismay, the Narmada Valley Development Project now envisages thirty-two thousand dams on the Narmada River and her forty-one tributaries. Thirty of the dams will be large, three hundred fifty medium sized. These dams will affect the lives of an estimated twenty-five million people in the valley. The first dam on the Narmada River, the Bargi Dam, completed in 1990, submerged three times more land than the engineers said it would and displaced 114,000 people from 162 villages. These people received little restitution or rehabilitation. While a few got a small cash compensation, most got nothing. Some of these villagers died of starvation. Other villagers moved to slums in the city of Jabalpur.

The Bargi Dam irrigates only the same amount of land it submerged, less than five percent of the amount of land the planners of the dam said it would irrigate. The Indian government claims there is no money to construct canals to bring the water from the river to the fields, even though it seems to have enough money to begin work downstream on the huge Narmada Sagar Dam.

The largest dam in the Narmada plan, the Sardar Sarovar

Dam, now under construction, will displace an estimated forty thousand to forty-two thousand families, or about two hundred thousand people. But according to the Narmada Bachao Andolan (NBA), a grassroots group protesting the dams, the actual number of affected families will be about eighty-five thousand, or close to a half million people.

I got used to small-time corruption while in India, such as paying for a driver's license without a test, but the large dam construction in India apparently is big, big-time corruption. Some of the canals associated with the new dams are never completed. Building costs are in some cases ten times more than budgeted. Most horrifying, however, is the ruining of the lives of the displaced villagers.

Despite this corruption, positive changes have taken place. While India might appear frozen in time, retaining many of its thousands of years of customs and traditions, major advances have been made in the areas of science and technology. Dramatic social changes also have occurred. President K.R. Narayanan, the current president of India, was previously a member of the "Untouchable" caste.

What I remember most about India, and find profoundly endearing, are the people, especially those in the rural areas. I was moved by their spirituality, the acceptance of their *karma* (fate), their respect and reverence for elders, their sense of gratitude, and their generous hospitality. They are what made the five years I spent in India the best five years of my life.

Sol Resnick

Tucson, Arizona • May 2001